Routledge Revivals

Medieval Islam

The history of Islam runs without a break from its origins to the present. Therefore, understanding medieval Islam gives us a much clearer comprehension of the modern world.

First published in 1979, this concise account of the Islamic world in the middle ages covers a vast territory, stretching from Morocco and Spain to India and Turkestan. It discusses the teachings of Islam, its theology, mysticism and philosophy, and examines the relation between Islam and political order, particularly the concepts of power and the organisation of government. It discusses Islam's view of the social order and concludes by looking at the urban centres in which Islamic civilisation developed, describing the towns themselves and the various forms of Islamic art.

This book will be of interest to those studying medieval and Islamic history.

Routledge Revivals

Medieval Islam

Dominique Sourdel
Translated by J. Montgomery Watt

Routledge
Taylor & Francis Group

First published in 1979 as L'Islam Médiéval
by Presses Universitaires de France
This translation first published in 1983
by Routledge & Kegan Paul Ltd

This edition first published in 2017 by Routledge
2 Park Square, Milton Park, Abingdon, Oxon, OX14 4RN
and by Routledge
711 Third Avenue, New York, NY 10017

Routledge is an imprint of the Taylor & Francis Group, an informa business

A Library of Congress record exists under LC control number: 83004431

ISBN 13: 978-1-138-06374-7 (hbk)
ISBN 13: 978-1-315-16080-1 (ebk)
ISBN 13: 978-1-138-06376-1 (pbk)

Medieval Islam

Dominique Sourdel
Translated by J. Montgomery Watt

First published in 1979 as L'Islam médiéval
by Presses Universitaires de France

This translation first published in 1983
by Routledge & Kegan Paul Ltd
First published as a paperback 1985
paperback reprinted 1986

11 New Fetter Lane, London EC4P 4EE
Published in the USA by
Routledge and Kegan Paul Inc
in association with Methuen Inc
29 West 35th Street, New York NY10001

Phototypeset in Linotron Bembo by
Input Typesetting Ltd, London
and printed in Great Britain by
T. J. Press (Padstow) Ltd., Cornwall

Library of Congress Cataloging in Publication Data
Sourdel, Dominique.
Medieval Islam.
Translation of: L'Islam médiéval.
Bibliography: p.
Includes index.
1. Islamic Empire. 2. Islam—History. I. Title.
DS38.3.S6313 1983 909'.097671 83–4431
ISBN 0–7100–9453–1 (c)
ISBN 0–7102–0883–9 (pb)

Contents

Introduction

The term 'Islam', as everyone knows, signifies 'submission to God', and, as such, essentially designates a *religion*, that which was preached by Muhammad (or Mahomet) at the beginning of the seventh century of our era in Arabia, and which then spread in the numerous countries conquered by the Muslim Arabs during the seventh and eighth centuries. The vast territory, where Islam thus prevailed, established itself as very different from those territories situated on its frontiers and with whom it was more or less in relation, and in particular very different from the Byzantine and European areas where Christianity held sway, as well as from the Asian complex in India and Turkestan which kept its ancient traditions; it was so different that the term *Islam* also came to be applied to a *world* whose history was marked by progressive development towards a true *civilisation*. This explanation satisfies by its simplicity, but would not however, by itself alone, account for the entire evolution of the facts. The reason for this is twofold. The first is that Islam as a doctrine never presented itself in a permanent and monolithic form but always bore within itself divergent currents of thought, and these have had varying success according to the period and did not fail to develop through mutual contact. The second is that the phenomena influenced by this doctrine have been conditioned equally by factors other than religious or intellectual. Thus it appears essential today to substitute, for any global explanation of Islamic civilisation, a more complete and delicate vision which makes it easier to state for each period and each field, whether political, social or economic, at what level was produced the influence of the doctrine which constantly inspired this civilisation and what aspect this influence assumed in each case.

The question of the origins of Muhammad's preaching at first raises controversies both old and contemporary, bearing on the specific nature of this monotheistic religion, but also showing the ambiguity of the character of its founder, which has been variously interpreted. To the variety of response which it arouses there is opposed the unanimity with which each individual recognises the universalist and conquering nature of Islam, whose expansion none the less is a problem for the historian. The latter in fact remains always inclined to ask if the phenomenon of the conquests is explained by the dynamism alone of the new doctrine or whether it was facilitated by contingent causes, and to ask also what sort of symbiosis was operating among the Muslim conquerors and the conquered peoples, whether converted to Islam or not.

The world thus constituted falls from then on within a definitive geographical framework, where factors of unity, but also of diversification, are manifest, which it is more fashionable than ever to discuss in order to try to evaluate the respective results. Added to this will be the effects of the continual transformations which later continued to affect this world in the course of centuries, and which it would be useful to examine to see whether they had direct or indirect relations with the very nature of Islam.

But the whole of the civilisation at first rests on a body of teaching whose components must be known. People have begun to say, in recent years, that at the beginning of Islam one had witnessed a progressive religious development which had an effect on political and social life, while at the same time being conditioned by certain features of the last. The process of formation of various currents of thought must thus be tackled, while taking into account external influences which could have contributed to mould them. As for the political order which was based in part on the theoretical constructions of the jurists, it also appears as the result of temporary necessities of organisation, and the fruit of ancient legacies confronted by the reflections which were provoked by these legacies themselves and which shaped for the most part the demands of Islam in the matter.

The social order, for its part, should not be considered as a block. It underwent transformations while also presenting a distinctive mark which has more to do, at the second degree it seems, with the civilisation sprung from Islam than with the religious doctrine itself. Finally, the urban centres in which this civilisation preferred to express itself, and where an art revealed itself which may be considered as new despite its numerous borrowings, witness in the same way to the complexity of the influences which combined to produce a world which to this day merits the designation 'Islamic'.

In addition, the remarks which follow and which are accompanied by a chronological table allowing the reader to find his bearings roughly among the dates and facts, apply primarily to a period extending to the Mongol invasion of 1260. This last event had in fact for its result the sanctioning of an explosion, towards which for some time already the Arabo-Islamic world had been moving, and whose climax was brought nearer by each new foreign invasion. The three cultural regions which from then on became separate, then developed clearly each at its own rhythm. These were the Turkish region, centred from now on in Anatolia, the Iranian region, extending into India, both having a future destiny distinct from the Arab or Arabised region, which persisted only in the Near East and the Maghrib. It may be conceded that from this moment the problems of civilisation in an Islamic environment presented themselves in a different fashion, which justifies the division we have seen good to adopt, but which should not however disguise the durability of many of these cultural constants, which authorises us still to search among medieval realities for the deep explanation of features of the contemporary world.

Chronological Table

	The West	*Middle East*	*Iran, Central Asia*
612		Beginning of Muhammad's preaching in Mecca	
622		The Hijra (Hegira)	
630		Return of Muhammad to Mecca	
632		Death of Muhammad	
632		632–4 Caliphate of Abu Bakr	
634		634–44 Caliphate of 'Umar Conquest of Syria and Mesopotamia	Beginning of the conquest of Iran
641		Foundation of Basra and Kufa	
642		Conquest of Egypt; foundation of Fustat	
644		644–56 Caliphate of 'Uthmān	
646	Beginning of the conquest of the Berbers		
651		The standard Koranic text established	Completion of the conquest of Iran
656		656–60 Caliphate of 'Ali	

Chronological Table

	The West	*Middle East*	*Iran, Central Asia*
660		660–750 *Umayyad dynasty* 660–80 Caliphate of Mu'āwiya	
661		Death of 'Ali at Kufa	
670	Foundation of Cairouan		
680		Death of al-Husayn at Kerbela (Iraq)	
685		685–705 Caliphate of 'Abd al-Malik	
691		Dome of the Rock, Jerusalem	
705		Foundation of Wasit in Iraq	
705		705–15 Caliphate of al-Walīd I Grand mosques of Aleppo, Damascus, Medina	
710	Completion of the conquest of the Berbers 710–16 Conquest of Spain		
714	Muslim raids into France		
724		724–43 Caliphate of Hishām	
732	Battle of Tours (or Poitiers)		
750		750–1260 *'Abbāsid dynasty* 750–4 Caliphate of al-Saffāh	
754		754–75 Caliphate of al-Mansūr	Victory of Muslims over Chinese at Talas Paper factory at Samarkand
756	Umayyad emirs of Cordova		
761	Rustamid emirs in the extreme Maghrib		

Chronological Table

	The West	*Middle East*	*Iran, Central Asia*
726		Foundation of Baghdad	
772		Foundation of Raqqa	
785	Great Mosque of Cordova		
786		786–809 Caliphate of Hārūn al-Rashīd	
789	Idrīsid emirs in the extreme Maghrib		
800	Foundation of Fez Aghlabid emirs in Ifriqiyya		
813		Siege of Baghdad 813–33 Caliphate of al-Ma'mūn	
821			821–73 Tāhirid emirs in Khorasan
831	Conquest of Palermo and of Sicily		
832		House of Wisdom at Baghdad; Mu'tazilite Inquisition	
836	Great Mosque of Cairouan	Recruitment of a guard of Turkish slaves Foundation of Samarra, the new capital	Campaign in Azerbayjan against the rebel Bābak
847		847–61 Caliphate of al-Mutawakkil	
864	Great Mosque of the Zaytuna at Tunis		
867			867–911 Saffārid emirs in Sistan, then Khorasan
868		868–905 Tūlūnid emirs in Egypt	
869		869–83 Revolt of the Zanj in Iraq	
873		Disappearance of the Twelfth Imām of the Twelver-Shī'a	

Chronological Table

	The West	*Middle East*	*Iran, Central Asia*
875			875–1005 Samānid emirs in Transoxiana, then Khorasan
883		Abandonment of Samarra as capital	
894		*Carmathian state* in Bahrein	
908		908–32 Caliphate of al-Muqtadir	
909	Conquest of Ifriqiyya by the Fātimid Mahdi 909–1171 *Dynasty of the Fātimids*		
912	912–961 Reign of 'Abd al-Rahmān III in Cordova; from 929 caliph		
922		Execution of al-Hallāj	
929		929–1004 *Hamdānid emirs* of Syria	
935		935–69 *Ikhshīdid emirs* of Egypt	
936		First 'great emir' in Baghdad	
945		945–1055 Būyid emirs in Iraq and in western Iran	
969		Conquest of Egypt by the Fatimids Foundation of Cairo	
972	972–1152 Zīrid emirs in Ifriqiyya	Great mosque of al-Azhar in Cairo	
992			992–1211 *Qarakhanid emirs* in Transoxiana
998			998–1186 *Ghaznavid emirs* in eastern Iran in Afghanistan
1001			1001 Conquest of the Punjab
1010	Break up of Islamic Spain		

Chronological Table

	The West	*Middle East*	*Iran, Central Asia*
1032			Appearance of Seljūqs in Transoxiana
1036	1036–1147 *Dynasty of the Almoravids* in the extreme Maghrib		
1041	Zīrid emirs recognised the Abbāsid caliph		
1052	Invasion of Ifrīqiyya by the Banu Hilāl		
1055			1055–1157 *Dynasty of the Seljūq sultans* in Iran, Iraq, then Syria
1061	1061–91 Loss of Sicily		
1062	Foundation of Marrakesh		
1071		Conquest of Anatolia by the Seljūqs	
1077		1077–1307 *Dynasty of the Seljūqs* of Rūm in Anatolia	
1099		Capture of Jerusalem by the Crusaders	
1127		1127–81 Dynasty of the *Zangid emirs* in Syria	
1130	1130–1269 *Dynasty of Almohads* in the Maghrib		
1141			Appearance of the Mongols in Transoxiana
1147		Second Crusade	
1150			1150–1215 *Dynasty of* the Ghūrids in Afghanistan and India
1156			1156–1231 *Dynasty of Khwarizmshahs* in Iran

Chronological Table

	The West	*Middle East*	*Iran, Central Asia*
1171		1171–1260 *Dynasty of the Ayyūbids* in Egypt and Syria	
1180		1180–1225 Caliphate of al-Nāsir in Baghdad	
1188		Recapture of Jerusalem by Saladin	
1206			1206–1555 *Dynasty of the Sultans of Delhi*
1216	Appearance of *Merīnid emirs* in the extreme Maghrib		
1230	1230–1492 *Dynasty of the Nasrid emirs* of Grenada		
1237	1237–1574 *Dynasty of the Hafsid emirs* of Tunis		
1243		Invasion of Anatolia by the Mongols	Domination of Iran by the Mongols
1249		Seizure of power in Egypt by the *Mamlūk sultans*	
1258		Occupation of Iraq and Syria by the *Mongols*	
1260		End of the dynasty of 'Abbāsid caliphs	

CHAPTER I

Islam – a monotheistic and universal religion

Islam is first of all both a universal religion and a religion of conquest, whose sudden rise in the seventh century of our era was followed by slower, but still constant expansion. Because of this, Islam had a doctrine whose successive and concomitant developments were bound up with political and historical events, and these will engage us a little further on. Because of this also, Islam remained faithful to a message which it never ceased to defend, that of a monotheistic religion, the third to assert itself after Judaism and Christianity; it wanted at one and the same time to follow these and to distinguish itself clearly from them, while only partially recognising their validity. To the Prophet of Islam was indeed said to have been delivered in its integrity the message which had been received earlier by Abraham but which had subsequently been distorted by those responsible for transmitting it after him.

This explains why it is appropriate first of all to show Islam's relation to the two great world religions which it sought to replace and with which its development brought it alongside and even into confrontation. This procedure corresponds to the attitude of the orientalists who could never study truly Islamic phenomena without making assertions about their origins. They did this in terms necessarily different from those used by Muslims; but it is interesting to discover, under their divergent and sometimes contradictory interpretations, the fundamental data which they borrowed from Islamic tradition itself and which they were content to consider in a completely different perspective.

1 Islam in relation to Judaism and Christianity

The position of Muslim believers is indeed very simple when they identify their faith with the original monotheism of the Biblical prophet Abraham, who is depicted by the Koran as the founder of the sanctuary at Mecca, the Ka'ba, and at the same time as the destroyer of idols and the father of Ishmael in whom the Arabs see their common ancestor. Not only does Abraham occupy a privileged place among the various prophets mentioned in the Koranic text, but the traditional accounts locate the sacrifice of his son in the region of Mecca; this is briefly alluded to in the Koran and it is also evoked very specially by one of the rites of pilgrimage which has been celebrated through the centuries with increasing solemnity.

This locating in the Hijaz of an Abrahamic tradition claimed as an Arab patrimony did not prevent Muhammad's preaching from being linked with Jerusalem by the story of the 'night journey' which commentators very soon developed as an explanation of a Koranic verse. It was in that city on the site of the ancient Temple that Muhammad, miraculously transported, was supposed to have been taken up into Heaven where he was said to have met the prophets of the Old Testament. The same tradition going back, it appears, to 'biographies' (*sīra*) written at the beginning of the eighth century, makes Moses appear advising Muhammad during his ascension to ask God to lessen the number of daily prayers, which were thus reduced to five. In addition Moses, transmitter of the first revealed Book which the Koran claims both to confirm and replace, would often appear in various *suras*: one reads for example (Koran XLVI, 12), 'Before this Book there was the Book of Moses . . . and this Book confirms it in the Arabic language.' Along with him other

Biblical prophets appear, each in the anecdotal context of the environment where he was said to have lived and where his story was supposed to have unfolded itself. They were nearly always considered to have delivered to their people by God's command a message which remained generally not understood.

The background of Biblical characters common to Islam, Judaism and Christianity is completed, according to Muslim belief, by the presence among them of Jesus whom the Koran holds equally to be a prophet: it recognises indeed the historic existence of the Son of Mary and admits his Virgin Birth, conferring on him the superior rank of bearer of 'the Spirit of God' while being quite unable to see in him the Son of God and to admit the event of his Crucifixion. This respect for the person of Jesus is combined with very hard sayings directed against the Christians who were held to have abandoned the true doctrine and to have adopted an 'associationism', idolatrous in the eyes of Muslims, in which can be seen a misunderstanding of the dogma of the Trinity. It is in this sense that Islam did not cease to number itself with the old monotheistic religions, whose adherents, or 'People of the Book', were held to have been the first to receive a message identical with that of Islam; this message was restored again in its purity only by the Koranic revelation whose divine origin forms the basis of all Muslim faith.

It thus seems natural in the eyes of the adherents of Islam that Muhammad should have been led to state precisely the position of the new religion in relation to a Christianity or a Judaism then represented in Arabia by more or less active believers. In fact there were said to have been at Mecca before the preaching of Muhammad some Christians of humble if not servile status, and there was said to exist at Yathrib, the future Medina, an important Jewish community with which the Prophet, installed as its neighbour after the Hijra, had soon quarrelled and which he ended by driving away or exterminating on a charge of treason. But Muslim opinion refuses to speak of any contingent influences which could then have affected Muhammad's thought, simple

'Messenger of God' and transmitter of an absolute truth by definition external to himself.

This position is evidently to be found only rarely among occidental scholars who hesitate to place the Koranic revelation 'after' revelations 'altered by their possessors'. On the contrary, indeed, when these scholars tried to underline the possible reconciliation between Muhammad's preaching and previous religious messages, they did so by falling more or less openly into religious polemic which is certainly not the domain of the historian but is one which he often finds it difficult to escape. Latent possibilities of conflict certainly exist and their existence is felt in some way or other by all those who interest themselves in Islam, betraying in this respect personal options and feelings which could have been distorted by modern intentions of a political character. Certainly it is useful here to mention some themes which have not ceased to nourish researches or discussions in this field and which make it possible at the same time to understand, behind the objective facts under review, a background of religious struggles still alive today after having largely determined certain confrontations of the medieval period.

Such conflicts arise out of external similarities which are apparent in all encounters between an Islam and a Judaism each relying on reverence for a sacred text which commentaries and collections of traditions have come to explain; in both cases religion does not consist in the imitation of a perfect model but in carrying out rules laid down by the doctors in religious sciences. Both doctrines, then, do not only carry articles of faith to which the believer must adhere but a social and moral code of life sometimes very precise, regulating in minute detail the actions of day-to-day living, notably according a primary importance to ritual purity and including some related prohibitions about food.

Hence the intensity of the problem set by the attitude of Muhammad towards the Jews of Medina whom he admitted at first to the bosom of his new community (their rights being recognised in the document wrongly called 'The Constitution of Medina') and whom he described afterwards as hypocrites, even traitors, and punished as such. That Muhammad may have had relations with these Jewish groups going beyond the framework of a simple political agreement is proved by the fact that the Prophet of Islam had from the very first ordered that the daily prayers be accomplished facing Jerusalem. The Koranic text mentions the obligation as well as the change which intervened when Muhammad replaced the 'direction of Jerusalem' by the 'direction of Mecca and the Ka'ba'.

So the Islamists are often asked about the meaning of this 'change' in the Koranic revelation and they have tried to place it in its religious context, that of the various *suras* which have been traditionally attributed some to the Meccan, some to the Medinan period of the Prophet's life. Certain people have thought they could discern in this respect an evolution by virtue of which the figure of Abraham took on an increasing importance while Mecca became the point towards which the believers had to turn in prayer and while Muhammad, separating himself from the Jews, began to attack them violently. Muhammad, as the Dutch scholar Wensinck following Snouck-Hurgronje wrote, 'was able to free himself from contemporary Judaism by attaching himself to the Judaism of Ibrahim [Abraham], which Judaism was the forerunner of Islam.' In the same way, the Englishman Torrey spoke of a 'Jewish Foundation of Islam' and the French Jesuit Lammens did not hesitate to describe Islam as the 'Arab adaptation of Biblical monotheism'. Similarly, the German Harnack declared 'Islam is a recasting on Arab soil of the Jewish religion after the Jewish religion had undergone an analogous operation through contact with a Judaising, gnostic Christianity.'

Recently this hypothesis has again been taken up of a role exercised by Judaeo-Christianity in the development of Islam, but it has been mostly in the field of research into the evolution of Judaism during the first centuries of the Christian era. The question has been asked whether Islam had characteristics in common with a Jewish sect, that of the Ebionites, who revered Christ as a prophet but not as the Son of God; or whether it was related to certain gnostic sects which regarded the Biblical prophets as the successive transmitters of the same message. There are some specific elements there which give pause for thought but whose importance one must be careful not to exaggerate on the basis of comparisons bearing only on limited points. Our knowledge of the religious movements situated on the periphery of Judaism and of Christianity during the century which preceded the appearance of Islam still remains too fragmentary for us to argue in a valid fashion about them.

Difficulties of the same order are not slow to appear when Christianity in turn is brought face to face with Islam. Certainly the doctrine which one can trace through Koranic preaching bears elements which are not original to it, such as the announcement of the Last Judgment or certain features of its angelology and demonology. God is surrounded by angels among whom some have been degraded for having refused to prostrate themselves not before God, but before man, and have thus become demons. The Judgment will separate humans into two categories, the elect who will enjoy Paradise and the damned who will be thrown into Hellfire.

To these may be added similarities of religious sentiment and of forms of piety which are thought to have been discovered between Oriental Christians and the first Muslims, and on which the Swede Tor Andrae, author of two classic works which appeared between 1918 and 1926, was one of the first to insist. He showed how the Syrian preachers well before Muhammad liked to describe the punishments endured by the peoples who had refused to follow their own prophets, or the penalties threatened after the Judgment to all those who had neglected the worship of God and the practice of alms-giving; and he underlined the analogies of content between texts which, in order to suggest the delights of Paradise, used in the same way a metaphorical language designed to render intelligible what human understanding was unable to conceive. From these comparisons it has been concluded that Muhammad had been in contact with Syrian Christians and one might ask for example if the monk Bahīra who, according to the *Life* of Muhammad, is said to have met him in his youth at Bosra in Syria and to have discovered in him a future prophet, would not represent one of the anchorites who might have familiarised the young camel-driver, in search of religious certitude, with various points of their own doctrine.

The idea was apparently very old, since certain Christians of the seventh century, without going so far as to present Islam as an 'Arab adaptation' of Christianity, did not hesitate to rank it among the 'heresies' of this religion precisely because of the personality of Bahīra whom later Oriental Christian polemicists continued to charge. The points from which these polemicists argue, however, correspond only to resemblances of detail which are after all secondary, whereas Islam opposes the Christian faith on essential affirmations such as belief in the Trinity or ideas of original sin and redemption. Thus the foundation, on which are based the efforts of certain modern authors who have tried to equate the Christ of Islam with the Jesus of the Gospels, is a flimsy one. Their allegations seem to make light of the fundamental differences between Islam and Christianity, differences which do not always exclude possible borrowings from archaic forms of Christian doctrine, such as have recently been thought to be discovered in certain passages of the Koranic text with a strophic structure.

2 The originality of Islam

Beyond these varied hypotheses and despite doctrinal variations which showed themselves in the course of its history, Islam never ceased to affirm, by means of the Koran and by means of subsequent Muslim reflection, a coherence and convictions which are its own and which no one could contest from the standpoint of religious anthropology. As a strict monotheism it can be described as total submission to a Creator God who is all-powerful, all-knowing, omniscient and supreme judge, but also compassionate and merciful, as the formula of the *basmala*, so often repeated and written by Muslims, affirms. This mercy, however, does not go beyond a simple pardon for faults committed and in no way evokes the feeling of the same name which is at the root of Christianity, but which, for Muslims, would be incompatible with strict transcendence. Moreover, Muslim religious life is essentially characterised by respect for the revealed word and by the observance of prescribed acts, which, apart from the well-known obligations of prayer, fasting, legal alms, pilgrimage and holy war, comprise a number of different rules or recommendations of a moral, social and political nature. Among these rules are, for example, those which justify the existence of legal penalties, which authorise slavery and which set up an organisation of the family and marriage based on the rights of the individual, establishing strictly the rights of inheritance while excluding neither concubinage nor repudiation (divorce).

This originality has, moreover, held the attention and some modern historians have recently asked themselves not so much about the external religious influences which might explain the content of the Islamic message as about the manner in which the message itself would have been a response to the exigencies of the society of that period, thus appearing in some measure as the 'product' of the society which had received it. The Scottish scholar, William Montgomery Watt, was the first to raise this question not without attracting many criticisms and refutations. In fact, the novelty of his procedure had been to study closely and in depth the position at Mecca on the eve of the *Hijra* by attributing greater value than had been the case up till then to the stories recorded in the *sīra* or the life of Muhammad. He there discovered data, previously unused, about the mutual relations of the clans and about the state of social tension which had existed in a city made rich by commerce across the desert but marked by the disproportionate growth of the fortunes which the families of caravan traders had built up. This situation of conflict and instability called forth new religious preaching in so far as the bedouin morality of the preceding epoch no longer sufficed to protect the weak against the strong, nor the poor clans against the clans who had grown rich. The idea was not entirely new and Henri Lammens had already for example, much earlier, described Mecca as a 'merchant republic'. But William Montgomery Watt's researches made it possible to place Muhammad's enterprise at a moment of imbalance which broke the ancient relationships and put in question the traditional values linked with that condition.

In the same way, a study of the origin of the first converts showed that Islam had found followers above all in the humbler circles which were threatened by the expansion of the most powerful clans. The proclamation of the Last Judgment and the condemnation of the rich would thus have been addressed in particular to those who dominated the 'merchant republic' and profited from their activities. From there to say that the economic situation had determined the proclamation of the Islamic message was only a single step, which Montgomery Watt always maintains he had not taken; according to him, the appearance of Islam was a response to the aspirations of certain people in a situation marked by social change but this did not mean that it was the only response possible. The relationship established between Islam and the historical circumstances surrounding its birth could not then be confused with the outcome of an absolute determinism; the historian's only concern is to scrutinise as exactly as possible the nature of the connections which could have existed between the Koranic message and the economic and religious atmosphere which prevailed at Mecca at the time of Muhammad.

To demonstrate the reality of these connections, some have wanted to make use of what was known of personages prior to Islam, who, according to Muslim chroniclers, had been converted to pure monotheism and designated by the term '*hanīfs*' which was also applied to Abraham in the Koran. The aspirations of these *hanīfs* were said to have witnessed to a tendency aiming at replacing the innumerable gods of Arab paganism by a single God, a tendency which Islam came precisely to satisfy. But the existence of monotheistic beliefs not accompanied by the moral teaching which characterises the Koran is difficult to imagine in the Meccan situation: one can only suppose a slow evolution from Arab paganism leading little by little towards monotheism. This last hypothesis has certainly met with some approval and it has been recalled that at Palmyra, in an environment strongly Arabised and at the start of the Christian era, an altar had been dedicated to a single God, compassionate and merciful. Apart from the fact that no one knows precisely who were the worshippers of this god, the distance in space and time which separates Palmyra in the Roman era from Mecca at the beginning of Islam, is enormous. On the other hand, the very fact of the existence of the *hanīfs* hardly survives detailed examination of some ancient texts where the term appears: it would seem that the term may have been used to signify no more than 'Muslim' by the biographers of the Prophet, and 'pagan' by some pre-Islamic poets. In this case it would be the equivalent of a Syriac word of the same meaning and nothing would permit one to affirm that there really were, before the time of Muhammad, followers of monotheism designated by this expression.

There are many observations seeking to illustrate the obstacles one is up against when trying to make use of evidence provided by the ancient Arab biographers of Muhammad. Encouraged to present certain episodes in the life of their hero, notably his childhood, in a miraculous climate whose authenticity remains very dubious, they force themselves moreover to explain the slightest passages of the Koran, perhaps reconstructing, in their own way, facts which, according to them, would have served as supports for these revelations. Certainly we can accord them more credence as regards the composition of the tribes, the identity of the first Muslims and their personal rivalries, all of which information has rightly served as a base for the hypothetical historical reconstructions of Montgomery Watt. But the hypercritical position retains its supporters, and some, like Régis Blachère, have always preferred to challenge the historicity of the *sīra*, to rely solely on the data of the Koranic text, without however completely succeeding in the undertaking.

3 The personality of Muhammad

The personality of Muhammad has for its part often been appreciated in different ways. If it is no longer a question nowadays of considering Muhammad as an imposter, as did Voltaire, or of doubting his sincerity, as did more recently Henri Lammens, it is still the case that his personality continues to provide those who study it with somewhat enigmatic or ambiguous aspects and that all response to the questions thus raised consequently modifies the interpretation of the Koranic message which is adopted. These questions which appear especially in a climate of confrontation between Islam and the two other monotheistic religions which it claims to continue and complete, have themselves raised numerous polemics.

The two-fold fact is that Muhammad did not conduct himself entirely after the manner of the Biblical prophets and that, besides, he does not present generally to the eyes of Muslims the same moral perfection of character as Christ. As a prophet not 'inspired' but commanded to recite a text which God had 'dictated' to him by the mediation of the angel Gabriel, he was above all very soon the holder of a quasi-absolute authority, following on the decision he had taken when he failed to gain acceptance in Mecca to emigrate with his first companions and to install himself several hundred kilometres away in the future Medina. This emigration, or *Hijra*, made him a head of state and leader in war, taking political and military initiatives, launching expeditions against the Meccans, organising the community of 'emigrants' and their 'helpers', decreeing new legislation while continuing with his religious appeals, justifying Medinan organisation and legislation by revelations transmitted at the appropriate moment, and appearing above all as a man of action who did not hesitate to assume the responsibilities of power though most of his decisions were supposed to rest on instructions of divine origin.

That Muhammad had thus in almost all circumstances acted by virtue of the prophetic injunctions of which he made himself the guarantor, underlines the close link which, from that time on, existed in Islam between politics and religion. Rules of a social nature, such as those concerned with details of private life or those which determine penal law and which were all promulgated at Medina, were considered to be an integral part of the revealed text. By this fact they assumed an inviolable character which inevitably raised some problems in the course of history. The social order stemming from Islam and on which Islamic civilisation rested was, from the beginning, thought of as a definite order, inseparable from the divine gift which had given birth to it.

The fact that Muhammad had justified in the same way certain features of his own conduct introduced other questions which have not ceased to embarrass certain modern historians, all the more so since Muhammad sometimes took decisions which cancelled previous ones, as that of making believers pray towards Mecca instead of Jerusalem. Muhammad's attitude in his relation with the first Muslims or with his enemies at Mecca, in his personal bearing and in his political conclusions, varied in fact according to certain circumstances which have sometimes led people to describe him as opportunist. Now it is well known that the ideas of opportunism or of change do not agree well *a priori* with the idea of a message of eternal validity.

Muslims nevertheless admit these variations. They have developed a special science with the object of studying verses from the Koran called 'abrogating' and 'abrogated' while there was until the modern period no temptation to assimilate this development to a progressive explanation of data by definition inviolable. The position adopted was rather to invoke the arbitrary character of a divine will which no creature could call into question: with the idea of revealed text was thus combined that of the divine mystery, in whose name it becomes impossible to formulate the slightest criticism of the manner in which the message was transmitted nor of the behaviour of Muhammad himself.

The personal conduct of the 'seal of the prophets' none the less appeared to some, apart from its opportunistic aspect, as having at times offended the moral code commonly observed at that period in the West as well as in the East in Christian circles. Already in the course of the ninth and tenth centuries, Byzantine authors who wrote refutations of Islam, elaborated with some complacency on Muhammad's sensuality and on the different facts which could be quoted to support this, for example, when he did not hesitate to marry the wife of his adopted brother after having caused her to be repudiated by her first husband, or when he did not hesitate to take more legitimate wives than were authorised by the Koranic rules. This manner of behaviour would moreover have been considered shocking by his contemporaries, since it had had to be justified each time by the revelations on which Muhammad relied in matters concerning his private as well as his public life; a notable example was when he had to reconcile himself with his spouse Aisha after a moment of suspected infidelity. Add to this Muhammad's cruelty shown in the wars, his frequent recourse to political assassination, and the massacres ordered by him on certain occasions, like the massacres of the Jews of Banu Qurayza at Medina. These are features which do not help to glorify him as the model figure he never pretended to be and which in their turn have been the object of varied commentaries.

Those who, among modern authors and after the fashion of Montgomery Watt, regard Muhammad as a 'prophet' to be compared, in certain points, to the prophets of the Old Testament, feel the need to say that the moral code of Muhammad's time was not that of ours. Others, like Francesco Gabrieli, dwell further, when touching on the same problems, on the differences separating the Christian and Islamic worlds. They believe that one is dealing in Islam with extremely different concepts, at least in the early stages, from what could be Christian concepts: on one hand, the defence of the infant community justified its members in the use of all means, including individual and mass murders: on the other hand, the sexual moral code, which in any case did not always apply to marriages with mainly political motives, had no connection in the Arab world with what it later became in the Christian West.

Other historians have again, more recently, preferred to

present Muhammad as a 'founder of an ideology' and no longer as a 'religious genius' or 'prophet' as had generally been done previously. In this interpretation Muhammad set up a new system of values implying a certain religious conception and, above all, a new social order, for whose success he authorised recourse to all sorts of procedures and even the carrying-out of acts of vengeance which were not the sign of nobility of spirit. Thus Maxime Rodinson, who adopts this point of view, does not hesitate to assimilate Islamic preaching to one of these 'myths which merge into history and are backed up by force', myths against which truth is powerless. This last formula is, according to him, a precise allusion to the episode in which one of Muhammad's secretaries, 'Abd Allah ibn Sa'd, writing down at his dictation the text of successive revelations, was supposed to have made additions of his own which Muhammad did not detect, and from this fact to have doubted the authenticity of the message: Muhammad pardoned him with difficulty, but 'Abd Allah could not be won over again entirely to the cause of Islam. Reflections of the same sort have anyway caused Maxime Rodinson to throw into relief the political aspect of Muhammad's activity as leader of a party for whom moral and religious preoccupations, in the modern sense of the term, would have taken second place, especially during the Medinan phase of his activity.

Thus the picture one gets of the plans pursued by Muhammad and the conditions under which the Koranic text was received, do not cease to vary according to the personal choice of whoever is studying them. It is, however, now conceded by all that Islam in much of its religious doctrine and ideology has its own special character in spite of the influences it underwent, coming either from previous religions or from the political circumstances of its development. Muhammad thus appeared as an authentic founder of a religion whose personality, strong enough to leave a lasting impression on those who had known him, must be viewed independently of the systems of values generally referred to by the contemporary West to explain certain features.

His preaching had in fact been marked, though this point

should not be unduly stressed, by a combination of what we call the spiritual and temporal, the genuinely religious commands of Muhammad and his social regulations, his activities as 'armed prophet' or 'community leader'. He had to promise his followers, in order to ensure their sincerity and ardour, material success, including military success over their enemies, and beyond this the certainty of a future existence and eternal happiness. This leads to a religion narrowly bound to immediate political exigencies and a triumphant religion, showing itself as such in the early stages and continuing to appear so subsequently in almost constant fashion.

4 Islam – religion of conquest

A triumphant religion by definition, is Islam also a universal religion? The revelation 'in Arabic' which Muhammad had received was, for this reason, meant essentially for the Arabs of the peninsula, but had also to be proclaimed to others than those who had first heard it. To what extent was Muhammad aware of preaching such a universal message? This is a difficult question for the religious historian to resolve but which in fact has little concern for the historian as such. It is clear that Islam had, very early on, an expansionist drive which carried it far beyond the Hijaz territory and that Muhammad himself tried towards the end of his life to subjugate and convert non-Arabs by sending out expeditions which, though at first fruitless, were later resumed profitably by his successors.

Thus Islam, barely founded, appeared in the shape of a religion of conquest. Muhammad, in the space of a few years, had actually united all the tribes of Arabia with whom he had shared the new religion and on whom he had imposed his personal authority. This fragile conquest, momentarily in jeopardy after his death, was later consolidated by Abū Bakr who had gained by force the submission of the rebels of the so-called great apostasy and who had given material expression to this triumph by obliging them to pay legal dues or *zakāt*, that is to say, a levy on goods. The operation only served to continue that which had started in Muhammad's lifetime with the capitulation of the Meccans after hard battles waged for political and commercial pre-eminence after the 'emigration' to Medina. It was justified by the Koranic verses which recommend that infidels should be fought until they are converted, with the exception always of the possessors of a scripture, meaning essentially Jews and Christians, who might still enjoy the life of salvation on condition that they paid tribute. The verse containing this last stipulation was to serve as a rule for the status of non-Muslims in the future territories of Islam. At the same time, the obligation was affirmed to wage what is often called the 'holy war' but is better described as 'legal war'. This, carried on permanently against non-Muslims, has often been counted among the pillars of Islam.

At the level of facts there are, to begin with, the first small-scale expeditions directed by Muhammad himself outside Arabia, to the regions of the Syrian desert where the Arab tribes had been in the habit of infiltrating for many centuries and sometimes, in the course of these migrations, becoming Christians. These attempts were followed by those of his immediate successors, the four 'rightly guided' caliphs whom the disputed elections had allowed to seize power and who, continuing the policy thus started, annexed immense territories without great difficulty: the almost simultaneous conquest of Byzantine Syria and Sassanid Mesopotamia (636–41), the conquest of Sassanid Iran (642–50), the conquest of Egypt (642–6), the conquest of the Maghrib which was temporarily halted by the internal dissensions of the new Islamic state (670–707), the conquest of Spain (712–14), the invasion of Southern Gaul (717–32) and at the other end of the empire, the conquest of Transoxiana (674) and Sind (711). Everything happened very rapidly and a century after the death of the Prophet the main limits had been reached and in the West the movement began to surge back with the battle of Poitiers (or Tours), while in the East it slackened in the regions of Central Asia and India. In this area considerable progress was nevertheless registered a little later, since in the tenth century the Muslims gained possession of the entire Indian subcontinent of which previously they had only occupied a fringe, and about the same time affirmed their occupation of the Turanian steppes in spite of the growing pressure from Nomadic Turks surging back towards the West.

These conquests, the story of which seems a little tedious, are no less fundamental to our understanding since it is they which allowed the expansion of Islam as a universal religion simultaneously with the birth and spread of the civilisation bound up with it. Thus appeared the Islamic Arab society whose first area of expansion was an empire both arabised and islamised. But this phenomenon which they present has not failed to surprise a number of historians. How was such a large and rapid movement possible?

At first it must be stressed that the penetration of the Arab tribes into Syria and Iraq was not something new. It had begun a long time previously and the tribes wandering in northern Arabia had always been attracted by the fertile regions which bordered their desert territories; they reached them easily by certain natural depressions such as that of the Wadi Sirhan. There is no question here of discussing the theory according to which the Arabian peninsula was supposed to be the 'cradle of the Semites' who had poured in successive waves over a long period into the regions lying to the North. This theory, adopted for example by René Dussaud, has its protagonists as well as its opponents. But what is undeniable is the fact that in the Roman epoch there were already Arabs installed in Syria and Iraq: certain local dynasties were of Arab origin and some Roman emperors had Arabo-Syrian ancestors. Judging from proper names found in its inscriptions, Palmyra seems to have had a partly Arab population which worshipped its own gods in special sanctuaries. In the same period, the Nabateans had settled themselves in the territories of present-day Jordan, borrowing the Armenian script of the populations with whom they came into contact, carrying on trade, but also practising agriculture, and had formed a state which the Roman forces brought to an end in AD 106. Semi-nomads also appeared on the eastern edge of the present Jebel Druze, leaving behind rudimentary inscriptions in Arabic, but using the characters described as 'Safaitic'.

Later on, new Arab groupings served as a protection for the two opposing empires, the Byzantine and the Sassanid: they were the Ghassanids in Syria, found all along the line of the ancient *limes*, and the Lakhmids of Iraq with their capital at Hira. It appears that Hira was the centre in which was elaborated the new alphabet. This spread subsequently through a large part of the civilised world in the form of the Arabic script, a script whose exact origins are still not properly established but which was certainly related to the Semitic scripts of the sedentary peoples neighbouring the ancient Arabs, either the Nabateo-Aramean script or the Syriac script. Ghassanids and Lakhmids had certainly disappeared before the appearance of Islam, swept away by the Persian invasion of 540; but, at the time when Muhammad began his preaching, isolated Arab tribes had settled afresh both in the south of Jordan and in lower Iraq, and had more or less merged with the local population whose religion they sometimes adopted, abandoning the particularly severe conditions of nomadic life in order to profit from the resources of cultivated regions.

Seen in this way, the Islamic conquest takes its place naturally in the prolongation of an infiltration which was for a long time peaceful. It would even seem that the first expeditions led by the Muslims under the leadership or on the orders of Muhammad, might have had, as their main objective, to convert and integrate into the new state the Arab tribes who had emigrated and were already half-settled outside Arabia.

The success encountered by these expeditions, if not in Muhammad's lifetime then certainly under the first caliphs at Medina and particularly under 'Umar, explains why the movement grew so rapidly. However, it is still necessary to explain how the nomadic, lightly armed horsemen succeeded in such a short space of time in overrunning part of Asia, then North Africa and Spain; as occupying the major part of the Byzantine possessions, including regions of Anatolia which were thereafter the target of multiple incursions right up to the walls of Constantinople; and in overthrowing totally a Sassanid empire whose last ruler died after the final rout of his troops. Religious enthusiasm, the taste for razzia and the lure of booty, often quoted by some, does not explain everything.

There are two questions to consider here: on the one hand, to what was the immediate superiority of the invaders attributable, and, on the other, how did the conquerors get the conquered peoples to accept their rule? We are at a loss to know how to answer the first question because it will always be difficult to solve problems of military technique owing to the acknowledged lack of documentation in this area. The chronicles only provide approximate figures of the armies opposing one another, even if it is known that in Syria final victory came only after fierce battles. It would appear that the Arabs might on the whole have had the advantage of numbers; but it is likely that they owed their victories chiefly to their mobility when facing elements whose equipment though superior, was heavy and constituted a handicap in a war of movement, and also when facing fortified towns whose resistance behind their ramparts became precarious from the moment that continued infiltrations created insecurity around them. One must also take into account the state of the combatants; the local troops recruited by the Byzantine generals doubtless did not display excessive zeal in defending a régime with which their cause could hardly be identified, seeing that various quarrels divided the natives from the imperial occupying power.

What was true for the troops stationed in Syria and even in Egypt was certainly not true in the same degree for North Africa, where semi-independent chiefs had for long succeeded in rejecting Byzantine tutelage without, however, being entirely supported by the population. It was still less so in the regions of the Sassanid empire where, moreover, we know little of the real state of the resources or of the military organisation. But another factor must definitely come in here: the Sassanid and Byzantine armies, shortly before the appearance of Islam, had committed themselves to a merciless war from which they had emerged considerably exhausted and those who had shown themselves to be the most enterprising, that is, the armies of the King of Kings, who had for a moment succeeded in reconstituting the Achaemenid empire, had been obliged shortly afterwards to retreat on all fronts and undergo the consequences of this evident defeat.

Reasons varying according to the regions could have facilitated the advance of the Muslims who, in general, followed a sure and skilful method in their strategic progress; they proved everywhere their knowledge of the natural ways of access, knew how to moderate the seeming impetuosity of their march with a certain prudence, above all based their offensives on the preliminary establishment of support points and camp cities which served as winter quarters as well as being a permanent link with the centre of the empire at Medina. The personalities of some able soldiers must also be remembered. Their names have been retained by tradition and their action continued to show itself for a much longer time in the neighbourhood of the frontiers which were slow to become stabilised. Among them must not be forgotten the figure of caliph ʻUmar whose legendary zeal and authority had left their imprint, both militarily and administratively, on an organisation which he had always done his best rigorously to control and master.

It must be added that other elements, too, were responsible for the ease with which certain towns surrendered to the invaders. The populations of Byzantine Syria for example, were, as we know, very dissatisfied with the Byzantine rule which was imposed on them, and which expressed itself chiefly in fiscal demands held to be intolerable. Besides, these populations had adopted, from the religious point of view, Christian doctrines which did not conform with orthodoxy as defined by Byzantium. The Monophysite doctrine was there dominant and hostility to official theological formulas, which was usual, was without doubt based on a diffused feeling of discontent rather than on precise intellectual reasoning. In general, the eastern Roman Empire, whose dominion extended to Africa, was composed of provinces too various from an ethnic viewpoint and at the same time, too developed culturally to be able to remain for long under the domination of Byzantium. Their inhabitants, who had for many decades observed, and sometimes taken part in, theological quarrels, did not find themselves in a position to reject immediately as a new religion, what appeared to them rather like a simple sect of Christian origin, as some contemporary texts suggest. Thus no urban group in a Syria or an Egypt politically or religiously detached from Byzantium had serious reasons for not seeking, by a negotiated capitulation, some satisfactory arrangement permitting it at the same time to preserve the lives and goods of its members in the centre of the new régime which these latter themselves helped to make viable.

We do not know if similar factors commanded popular reaction at the centre of the Sassanid empire. But there, too, religious dissensions had for long raged and thrived from a real lack of interior cohesion. To official Zoroastrianism were opposed the Manicheism which, thanks to its dynamism, penetrated numerous groups, as well as the Mazdakism of a more social hue, not to mention the other religions and philosophical sects which succeeded in winning followers in the midst of various peoples scattered from the eastern regions of the Iranian plateau to the vast Mesopotamian plains. In this geographical mosaic, no real attachment appears to have been felt towards the Sassanid ruler and his court, whose fall would seem to have been received without displeasure. Thus it can be easily explained how Islam, after totally or in part destroying the Byzantine and Sassanid powers, expanded further both to the East and to the West, in a movement of continued growth of power whose chief stages of development we have looked at. Towards the year 750 the impressive empire which had submitted to the Arabs touched the Pyrenees on one side, and on the other, the Indus or the valley of the Oxus (Amu Darya). New waves of combatants passed even this last frontier to throw themselves against the Turks and, still further, against the Chinese who, in the mountainous passes of Ferghana, reached the furthest limits of their own territorial expansion.

5 Conquerors and conquered

This vast conglomeration of conquered territory, which in some respects formed a simple and heterogeneous sum of very diversified regions, all anxious to preserve as much as possible of their autonomy and of their ancient peculiarities was no less a domain unified by conquest and entirely ruled by Islam and the principles which the latter had, from the very first, inspired. The head of the community, the caliph, was the recognised leader. Next to him, the Muslim victors alone enjoyed, by definition, a privileged position, and the natives employed or retained in administrative jobs could not escape from the subordinate roles to which their ethnic origins condemned them, whether they were converted or not. Everything seemed so ordered that the hierarchy instituted by the military successes which reserved military functions and levers of command for the first Muslims, the Arabs, would remain that of the new world which had arisen out of this situation.

However, the established order quickly became modified in the direction of universalism; conversions multiplied and the new Muslims claimed the right to share in the responsibilities and profits; relations with the subject peoples, for the most part not Arab and not Muslim, soon posed problems whose solution, which turned out to be delicate, weighed on the future of the adopted forms of government and the social relationships linked with them; a sphere, both islamicised and arabised, was gradually formed, whose frontiers corresponded exactly to those of the *dār al-Islām* and whose internal difficulties rebounded on the emergent Arabo-Islamic civilisation.

What in fact had been the treatment of the inhabitants of the regions henceforth subject to Islam? The Arab chroniclers report that the towns and territories had been occupied, sometimes 'by force', sometimes by virtue of a treaty, and that their status varied according to the conditions of the conquest. But these conditions affected above all the status of the lands, which had been imposed according to different fiscal regulations, and did not have any real effect on the status of the people: in all these cases the followers of he so-called religions of the Book, Judaism and Christianity, to which were added Zoroastrianism and other Iranian religions, were able to keep security of life and freedom of worship because of very precise Koranic rules. The others, that is, the pagan Arabs of Arabia, for example, were quite simply reduced to slavery. Such was also the fate of the warriors made prisoners on the Asiatic frontiers of Transoxiana or India, prisoners of war who were always, as a general rule, fairly rapidly freed, and, from the moment they became converts to Islam, were accepted into the new society.

Thus three quite distinct categories were rapidly established in the midst of the peoples of the empire: the conquering Arab Muslims, the non-Arab converts, the non-Arabs who remained faithful to their original religion; but a process of assimilation made itself felt between these different elements. This process, which varied in intensity according to region and period, followed the steady progression of conversions to Islam which became more frequent when they allowed the interested party to acquire certain social advantages. If there was no conversion, the *dhimmis*, as they were called, formed separate communities somewhat on the margin of Islamic society. Their members had neither the same obligations nor the same rights as the Muslims, whether converted or not, but their legal existence was sufficiently recognised for them to form after a fashion in their own way a part of the world of Islam and for their members to have the opportunity to participate in no small way at the cultural level as well as in administrative practice.

The Arabic language had very soon spread among the conquered peoples, so much so that from the end of the eighth century, the Umayyad caliph, 'Abd al-Mālik, was able to proceed with the arabisation of the administrative registers previously written in their local languages, Greek, Latin or Pahlavi. In the same way, the currencies, which had until then imitated Byzantine or Sassanid coins, were struck according to new models which excluded any human representation and only bore Arabic inscriptions. It is true that this arabisation was not achieved immediately and the measures taken by the caliph needed some time, especially in the eastern provinces situated at a distance from the capital. But such a tranformation illustrates the first step in the assimilation of the natives.

The stages which followed, which concerned the army and the tax system, posed more delicate problems. It is true that the conquests had offered these non-Arab warriors certain possibilities of integration. Berber elements converted to Islam were thus admitted to fight in the Maghrib and these same Berbers took an active part, a predominant part some think with a little exaggeration, in the expeditions into Spain; it is a fact, for example, that the leader of the first victorious campaign in that country, a certain Tāriq, who is supposed to have given his name to Gibraltar, was a Berber. Such a situation only presented itself in the West. In the East, the Arabs for long remained the sole providers of men for the conquering armies and we have to wait until the beginning of the eighth century, with the organisation of the Abbasid revolutionary movement, for some Iranians of Khorasan to be admitted into the local troops in virtue of one of the claims which gave most support to anti-Umayyad propaganda. This was the first step and, after the success of the revolt and the overthrow of the dynasty, it was followed by their entry into the caliph's troops until another change intervened, and an 'Abbāsid army of mercenaries, originally slaves, appeared, whose importance in medieval Muslim society we shall see later.

Meanwhile more pressing difficulties, bound up even more with the stages of assimilation, had appeared in the domain of the tax-system. In fact the Muslims, subjected to the legal alms alone, paid at first only a small tax of the order of a tenth on the revenues of lands which belonged to them in Arabia, as well as on the domains which had been conceded to them in Syria or elsewhere. The *dhimmis*, on the contrary, had been immediately subjected to much more important taxes whose rates, which always tended to become uniform, had been fixed at the moment of conquest, varying according to the places and also according to circumstances which still remain obscure to historians; it would appear that the city dwellers had at first been obliged to pay a personal tax (or poll-tax) while the country dwellers had to pay a global tax corresponding to the extent of their lands but that the conversion of the parties did not result in any lightening of their dues.

The moment arrived, at the end of the seventh century, when the new converts, especially in Iraq, intended to be treated on an equal footing with the old Muslims and as a result no longer to pay the total sums formerly imposed on them. In order to escape their fiscal obligations, some even left the lands which they cultivated and helped to swell the population of the towns where they carried on a new trade. Faced with this rural exodus, the governors were forced to take drastic measures; the fugitives would have to go back to their lands but, in compensation, the tax due from them was slightly reduced. Thus it seems a distinction was begun to be made between the so-called personal capitation tax (or poll-tax) with its Koranic name of *jizya* and the land tax or *kharāj*.

These improvements made gradually in their initial status were not, however, sufficient to satisfy the converts called *mawālī* or 'clients' because at the time of their conversion they had been obliged to attach themselves as clients to some Arab tribe. In the Umayyad period they were not admitted, as we have seen, into the Syrian army and only some individuals from among them would have succeeded in gaining access to desirable positions in the caliph's entourage. Their discontent increasing with the conditions of life which were theirs, especially in the Iranian or Irano-Mesopotamian provinces, showed itself with particular force at the beginning of the eighth century, engendered dissension among the Arab groups supporting the Umayyad caliphs and was the chief cause of the fall of this dynasty, which moreover the descendents of the Hāshimite branch pursued with their rancour.

Certainly the victory of the 'Abbāsid partisans practically put an end to the difficulties thus raised. But the rivalry between Arabs and non-Arabs reappeared in a different form, the Iranians wanting to claim for themselves in some way the new emerging culture. One could not as yet know whether, while being modelled on Islamic rules it would be primarily Arabo-Islamic, based on Arab traditions, or whether it would develop into a much wider culture having recourse to various non-Arab traditions. The claims of the *mawālī* thus fuelled the dispute which was known as that of the *shu'ūbiyya* since it grew out of the claims of the peoples (*shu'ūb*), that is, the conquered peoples, to impose their moral and intellectual ideals.

Characteristic of this outlook was the attitude of Ibn al-Muqaffa', a newly converted Iranian and Zoroastrian secretary who, during the first 'Abbāsid reigns, translated the *Book of Kalila and Dimna*, a Pahlavi collection derived from the *Fables of Bidpai* and composed of treatises for the use of kings and courtiers which drew inspiration from Sassanian treatises of the same kind. The dispute which these treatises had started continued for the whole of the eighth century and until the beginning of the ninth century. In the end, a sort of compromise prevailed: if the Arab heritage was preserved, Iranian or Indo-Iranian wisdom as well as Greek wisdom (or what was considered such) happened to nourish Islamic thought in the same way as the tales going back to the ancient Arabs. Greek science and logic were also adopted thanks to a huge effort of translation encouraged by the caliphs at the beginning of the ninth century, which enabled Islamic thinkers to finalise their arguments in defence of dogma threatened by Iranianism.

Thus a culture gradually grew up which was enriched by various contributions while remaining tied in its development to different aspects of a doctrine to which we shall return later. It rested on the principles of Islam but in the domain of ethics and practical policy in particular made room for the foreign traditions of the conquered peoples, notably the Iranians. In it there was affirmed an Arabo Islamic unity which valued not only the universal application – though sometimes modified – of the same law and the everyday use of the Arabic language, but also the spread of a religious and moral reflection which was accessible to everyone and in all regions. Even the non-Muslims who provided such an important contribution to the task of translating the Greek works, were arabised and if certain communities preserved their primitive liturgical languages and sometimes a doctrinal literature in their own tongue (for example, the Christian communities using Syriac), they did not, however, neglect the knowledge of Arabic which they used as their everyday language and as a vehicle of culture.

It was the affirmation, present in the facts since the victorious expansion of the first Islamic years, of this vocation to universalism which is also attested by certain versions, doubtless late, of the discourse spoken by Muhammad shortly before his death. The religion of an Arab prophet who would none the less have proclaimed in his last personal message that all, Arabs and non-Arabs, were equal, had become that of a medieval empire whose originality, compared with the worlds of the Christian West or the Byzantine East, cannot be doubted by the historian. The evolution, however, was not achieved without some diminution of the supremacy at first accorded to the Arabs, but this came about, of course, to the extent that the problems of social organisation and cultural change, which we have just indicated, were gradually resolved.

Indeed their language, in so far as it was the scholarly and liturgical language, experienced a rejuvenation which has never been denied and which explains why it is still taught today for the religious needs of Muslims, in black Africa as well as in Iran, Afghanistan, and even India. But the Arabs themselves had none the less been gradually eliminated at the centre of the empire from all their important functions to preserve only an honorary role. The people chosen by virtue of the revelation having become a conquering people, were practically deprived of any directing role in the community now constituted. All that remained was the call of Islam to victory, a call which unfavourable historical circumstances sometimes placed on the level of a millenarian, or more rarely eschatological, hope, but which was always found ready to support the current ambitions of empire-founding rulers. It was at one and the same time the strength and weakness of a world where this call roused the aspirations of Muslims belonging to different regions and ethnic groups, the sources of a history where the ferments of revolt and of division often prevailed over the clear awareness of a socio-religious unity that was nevertheless real.

CHAPTER 2

The medieval Islamic world

The civilisation whose development is rightly attributed to the spread of Islam was due partly, as we have seen, to the activity of peoples from Arabia, whose victorious emigration was accompanied by a parallel expansion of their language and their tradition. But it also fitted into a geographical framework where the unity of countryside and modes of life in the medieval period can only seem surprising. Indeed, in spite of the huge area of a world which, on one side touched western Europe, on the other the borders of China and India, its main elements all, or nearly all, belonged to what we call the arid or subarid zone. This was country where the rainfall was, and still is, insufficient, where cultivation, more often than not, could only be done by irrigation, where wide spaces, which had remained steppe or desert, for long constituted lands propitious to nomadic life but with very noticeable variations according to time and place.

This is why historians and modern western geographers have not hesitated to try to match certain characteristics of the new civilisation with the environment in which it originated and developed, then to form hypotheses about the actions and reactions which were produced between different kinds of behaviour imposed by the very nature of the climate, and about the rules gradually worked out within the nascent Islamic society. It would be impossible to discuss here all these theories which sometimes contradict one another and often only look at one aspect of an evolution made extremely complex by the interaction of various influences. They must still be discussed briefly as so many lines of research insufficiently explored, and the powerful factors of the unity and the originality of the ancient Islamic world, to which the exploitation and commercialisation of natural resources were related, must no longer be neglected.

1 The influence of Arabia

Does the message of Islam in the first place owe something to the Arab peninsula and to the bedouin environment? Many have thought so while sometimes giving different answers to this question; the latest of these is that of Montgomery Watt already mentioned. But long before the orientalists, the Muslims had always had the conviction that Islam and Arabism got confused in the manifestations which followed the birth of the first Muslim empire as well as in the distinctive features of the state established locally by Muhammad at Medina in an Arab environment and as a response to Arab hopes.

It is in fact clear that Islamic preaching, at first directed at the Arabs of Arabia, had not been able to avoid taking account of their customs even though it had come to modify them. Again, one must not forget that these customs were not uniform in a population which, among people who, while coming from the same ethnic stock, included both the far-ranging and the less adventurous nomads, sedentary cultivators inhabiting the oases, and caravan people with urban connections, controlling the routes of the Hijaz: all of these were Arabs whose families, belonging to clans and tribes which boasted comparable genealogies, presented different customs.

It was therefore certainly necessary to emphasise the ambiguous relationship that the Muslim religion had maintained from its beginnings with the bedouin ideal and the exigencies of tribal life. Substituting the brotherhood of believers for the solidarity of the members of the same clan, condemning the materialistic and fatalistic spirit of the nomadic pastoralists as well as their desire for profit, while at the same time also opposing, as one has not ceased to repeat, the mercantile activity of the Meccan caravan organisers, Islam nevertheless had continued to favour, by the principle of the *jihād*, the practice of the razzia dear to the Arabs and had thus preserved in some aspects their warlike spirit.

There were also, however, the ancient traditions of urban life belonging to the Hijaz, notably in the 'merchant republic' of Mecca, and it is these which one has wanted to rediscover by making Islam an 'essentially urban religion' The fundamental observation in this respect, previously formulated by William Marçais who took up an idea expressed by Ernest Renan, was that certain ritualistic obligations characteristic of Islam – as they are defined by the Law in the form of prayers, ablutions, fasting, and wearing the veil for women – had been designed specially for people living in the towns: hence the preferential treatment always experienced in Islamic lands for the creation of urban centres.

These last assertions, often admitted by the geographers, always imply, on the one hand, that the Hijaz had known at the time of Muhammad centres of sedentary life deserving to be called urban; on the other hand, that the ritual obligations considered later as significant had been prescribed and observed from this period. Now these two assumptions are subject to caution. Can one in fact speak of the existence of a real urban environment either at Mecca, a simple caravan settlement, or at Medina, a rural collection of villages strung out along a series of oases? If, for Medina, the expression *madīnat* 'al-nabi' or 'of the Prophet' was used and includes a term *madīna*, which later had the meaning 'town', at this ancient period the term must be understood in a sense that only suggests its later use; it would merely have designated the place where there was the seat of the man with power, the arbiter of delicate situations, the one who dealt out justice (*dīn*) and who delivered sentence, as was the case with the Prophet. As to the principal ritual obligations, such as the practice of the five daily prayers which were not based on

Koranic injunctions, it is not known at what exact period they were rigorously observed.

Thus if it appears difficult to see an 'urban' religion in early Islam, one can, on the other hand, look to a characteristic of the life of that era for one of the causes of urban development which showed itself soon after the conquests in a way which cannot be denied. We know for a fact that the great merchants had recently arranged the passage of luxury items through the Hijaz from the ports of southern Arabia to those of the Mediterranean. Those who organised these caravans pursued their activities after the preaching of Islam, despite the threats that Muhammad imposed on those who were too greedy for riches, and various Companions of the Prophet are reputed to have given themselves over to commerce from the time of the Medinan community. It could be that such a practice, further facilitated by the emergence of the Arab Empire, had contributed for its part to the growth of the towns, and thus traced back to the great camel-drivers of the Hijaz one of the characteristics of the civilisation which grew out of Islam. Thus one would find, precisely in this example, an illustration of one of the assertions of the geographer Xavier de Planhol who reckoned, among the original characteristics of Islamic civilisation, the combination which permitted urban and nomadic groupings, each drawing on an original Arab tradition, to show themselves equally the agents of diffusion.

2 Urban development

Several cities were effectively founded on Islamic territory from the period of the conquests onwards; for example, Basra and Kufa in Iraq, Shiraz in Iran, Fustat in Egypt, Cairouan in Tunisia. It is true to say that these cities were at first only camp-cities, serving as departure bases for the contingents which left for the Sassanid or Byzantine provinces. But around the centres of sedentary life, which they could not fail to be for the Arabs, various elements of the local population whether converted or not, arranged themselves, while the conquerors or their descendants gave themselves over to new tasks as the profits from booty diminished; thus these first 'man-made cities' of Islam became commercial centres taking over from ancient metropolises while elsewhere, as in Syria, cities that were there before Islam kept their power to attract and absorbed newcomers. In both cases these cities benefited from both the commercial acumen of the first followers of Islam, and the resources of a territory henceforth crossed by trade routes made practicable despite distances by political unification. The Sassanid empire, to which could be added the Visigothic Iberian peninsula, from now on constituted only a single world where merchandise could circulate freely from Transoxiana or from Arabia to the Mediterranian coasts, from Egypt to the Maghrib and even to Spain.

This ease of exchange, bringing with it a constant demand for manufactured products which only the artisans of the towns were able to supply, assured above all in urban development that of the industrial and working-class quarters. It would not explain the proliferation of the other 'man-made cities' directly linked with the will of the various holders of power. Indeed, the Muslim rulers, whether caliphs or such of their representatives and local governors as had obtained in certain provinces a real and rapid autonomy, very soon had the desire to create sumptuous residences, where they lived surrounded by their guards, and where they united also under their control the administrative machinery appropriate to each capital or regional centre.

Alongside these seats of government, sometimes ephemeral but also capable of reviving at a short distance from one another with ever-renewed vitality on sites like those of Fustat, Cairouan or Delhi, there developed, generally at a second stage, commercial cities which profited by being near them but were equally able to outlive them if the site had been well chosen: to the creations of rulers who symbolically reflected their power in their royal foundations, spending on them the profit of their war-like enterprises and by their pomp attracting to them activities of all kinds, there followed quite naturally genuine metropolises of which the classic example is provided in Iraq by Baghdad.

There indeed, a 'round city' provided with a solid wall and celebrated by the Arab chroniclers, had been built in 762 by the second 'Abbāsid caliph, al-Mansūr, to shelter his palace. The merchant quarters, which had at first been planned, had later to move outside its gates, increasing the built-up area. A second royal residence was later created, on the other side of the Tigris, by the heir-apparent, al-Mahdi, in 868, a residence which in its turn formed the centre of an important city on the eastern bank of the river. Other aristocratic foundations were added to this and the prosperity which an ever-growing economic development brought with it, at the crossing of north-south and east-west trade routes, allowed it to become an enormous medieval conurbation. Certainly its decline could be felt from the moment that trade was no longer constantly stimulated by the needs of a court greedy for luxury. The impoverishment of the caliphs in particular, who were no longer the masters of real power after 945, hindered them from remedying the disasters caused by the wars or by natural catastrophes like floods. But the heart of the capital maintained itself none the less until modern times when its position found new favour.

The prestigious fate of Baghdad, identified even today in history and legend, with the 'Abbāsid city *par excellence* of the golden age, makes one forget the other residences of the caliphs in Iraq, for example, Raqqa on the Euphrates or Samarra whose name and ruins appeal specially to archaeologists. For its part, Basra in the Middle Ages experienced a remarkable development because of its position as a port open to the Far East at the mouth of two Mesopotamian rivers, while Kufa suffered from the rivalry of Baghdad which was too near and was favoured by political circumstances. But the other large city of the Islamic Middle Ages must be looked for in Egypt where Fustat had soon eclipsed Alexandria, as well as the ancient Babylon, opposite which it had been built. A commercial city rich in the produce of its hinterland, it was extended towards the North by new 'residential' and royal quarters built by the 'Abbāsid governors, or by the autonomous Tulūnid emirs who, towards the end of the ninth century, wanted to create their own city there. It subsequently preserved its key role right up to the time when the foundation of the Fātimid caliphs, al-Qāhira (Cairo) created from scratch still further north in 969, at the moment of their triumphant installation in the East, received in its turn industrial and commercial activity which was never again to desert it, even after the abandonment of its royal palaces and the establishment of the new Ayyubid residence at the centre of a strong citadel dominating the conurbation.

Still further west, the same movement could be felt. Not only was there the town of Cairouan, which too had appeared as a camp-city of the period of conquest and for long preserved its character as chief town of the province marked by the juxtaposition around it of several government towns, one flourishing after the other; but other cities called to an enduring future were created in their turn in the furthest Maghrib, by the will of rulers belonging to successive dynasties. Thus Fez and its double conurbation came into being about 808, Marrakesh about 1062, both of them, but particularly Fez, owing their continuing future to the crossing of trade routes.

In Spain, on the other hand, where the only new towns founded were on the coast (Almeria, Murcia), the ancient cities retained their pre-eminence, sometimes with the development, as at Cordova, of grandiose palatial dwellings in their immediate neighbourhood. And the position was even more complex at the other end of the world of Islam on the Iranian plateau, where, through an absence of camp cities, we find, alongside some new creations, the ancient Iranian cities hastening their expansion by adding, to their pre-existing centres, quarters which were related both to the influx of Arab conquerors and to the growth of economic life. Sites long since inhabited like those of Nishapur, Merv or Samarkand, were soon housing veritable metropolises; the town of Shiraz grew out of an Islamic military colony; others grew up around the royal palaces of Ghazni or Bust-Lashkari-Bazaar in the high valleys of the Hindu Kush or the irrigated lands of Sistan; and Meshhed eventually developed, at the beginning of the ninth century, around a much-venerated mausoleum, so that it soon came to take the place of the neighbouring town of Tus, while two twin localities in the oasis of Isfahan merged to make way for a unique capital which soon became very prosperous and more and more vast.

Thus Islam's domination was expressed either by a multiplication in the number of towns or by an undeniable growth in population and area of ancient cities now occupied by the conquerors, whether it was in Egypt, in the Maghrib, or in Spain, as in Syria, Iraq or Iran. But the reasons leading to this evolution were sometimes varied, as we have seen, indeed as varied as the character of the towns which went from the palace-town to the commercial city, and which underwent the effects of both natural conditions and the repercussions of particular historical events. Nevertheless the tendency towards urban development did not go unchecked, witness the frequent examples of towns soon ruined and turned back into desert which can be counted today in the Islamic world. Similarly we do not know the exact thread of cause and effect between the Islamic religion and the blossoming of an urbanisation which was in fact a response to the play of multiple factors.

Certainly the famous towns, whether towns of government or active metropolises, were also intellectual centres where doctrine was elaborated and taught, and where secular disciplines were similarly studied. It has often been observed that the 'histories' of these towns which were written in the course of the Middle Ages almost always take the form of collections of biographical notices either about the scholars who taught there, or about the rulers and emirs who stamped their personalities on them. But at that point we are talking about consequences rather than about causes of urban development; and the centres of studies owing their origin to patronage, which came into existence in political centres which we shall later see to be fused with centres of civilisation, gave prestige only to cities already developed.

It was with difficulty, for example, that the scholars of

Kufa managed to maintain their independence over against the schools in the large metropolises of Basra and Baghdad which were favoured for reasons quite other than religious. The only instances of towns emerging from Islam and for Islam are those of the large built-up areas around a sanctuary or a place of pilgrimage like Meshhed and Qumm in Iran, or Kerbela and Nejef in Iraq.

Apart from such reasons, the importance assumed by the towns in the medieval Muslim world must stem, in a more general manner, from the opposition which then existed between the refinements of urban life and the isolation to which the inhabitants of the steppes and countryside were reduced; for the latter were without security yet always ready to come and sow trouble in the opulent cities. These are the geographical realities of arid countries, accompanied simply by the considerations pertaining to each particular case. They would have to be referred to in order to give an account, with some hope of success, of the evolution of Islamic towns, since each had its history and its profound originality, although their cyclic rhythm of development has some resemblance to that which governed relations in the same regions between nomads and sedentary peoples. These we must now consider.

3 Nomadism

The question of nomadism and its extension in some Islamic countries where it sometimes brought with it changes and catastrophes demands equally a certain prudence when one approaches the realm of hasty generalisations which one has too often accepted. It is true that the Muslim conquerors were largely former nomads or semi-nomads who did not immediately abandon their customs in the places where they settled. But they do not seem to have transformed, at the moment of conquest, the regions which they took over, and most of the 'Arabs', having then colonised the conquered territories, rapidly became sedentary. The primitive 'camps' thus became very quickly the living conurbations which we have just mentioned, while the rural properties deserted by their former owners revived to the profit of new masters. Certainly, to belong to an Arab tribe remained for two or three centuries a sign of pride, so much so that, as we have seen, the first converts attached themselves by the bond of clientship to a tribe, but this concern did not imply a real attachment to such bedouin customs as continued only in limited groups.

The situation later developed differently according to the regions, the relevant ethnic substrata and the effects of subsequent invasions; but the problem remains of knowing whether the Islamic period was characterised everywhere by a progressive diminution of arable areas. It has been thought possible to give an affirmative answer to this last question in the case of Iraq, where recent exact archaeological researches have allowed it to be established that the irrigated lands were less important at the beginning of the 'Abbāsid era than in previous eras. But the fact thus attested does not in itself imply that the Muslim conquerors had voluntarily neglected both agriculture and the upkeep of the canals. Rather it would appear that other causes played their part, such as the impoverishment of the soil or the effects of certain technical difficulties that arose by chance.

In the same way we cannot draw conclusions from the fact that, shortly after the conquest, the lands may have been cultivated especially by natives who, remaining faithful to their original religion, chiefly Christianity and Zoroastrianism, were consequently treated as second-class. Certainly the new 'feudal lords', if one may apply that term to the persons who benefited from the right to the tax and who were the possessors of these same lands, sometimes with a provisional title, did not live on these estates and had no direct personal link with the agricultural origin of their revenues. This situation, however, did not prevent them from being concerned about them and, from the beginning of the eighth century, large landowners, for example, tried to improve the unsatisfactory methods of exploiting their estates, as is learnt from the stories of the period and by examining regions now desert. Certain princes even expended great efforts in trying to bring estates into good condition; some drained marshlands like those of the Batā'ih of lower Iraq, following the example of the celebrated Maslama, son of the caliph 'Abd al-Malik, and others developed around their residences in the Syrian 'desert' hydraulic networks whose remains have claimed the attention of an archaeologist like Jean Sauvaget. Such works, if they were to be eventually profitable demanded financial means which only the members of great families had at their disposal. They show that the cultivated lands were far from being neglected by an Arab-Muslim aristocracy which pursued a policy similar to that of its predecessors in the same regions, a policy practised equally in other less central provinces and which lasted during the whole of the first period of 'Abbāsid rule.

Thus not only did the caliph in fact own personal domains in Iraq and in Syria, whose revenues fortified his coffers; but the military leaders and the dignitaries or servants of the State relied equally on the yield from the harvests and these proceeds added to their normal income. Thus if the high society whose members gravitated around the 'Abbāsid court was not, properly speaking, landowning, its standard of living was bound up with the prosperity of the lands at its disposal, both at the centre of the empire and in the regions where Muslim domination brought with it, for example, the introduction of new methods of cultivation or the harnessing of water for irrigation.

Add to this the fact that since the land taxes furnished the greater part of the state revenues, the central administration had to ensure the abundance of the harvests on which the taxes were based and this is proved by the reflections of certain viziers of the tenth century on the pernicious effect in the long term of too severe taxes. The justice of their observations in this respect does not mean that in a medieval Muslim context the rulers were always careful to treat the farmers well so as to ensure the yield of the lands; certain pressures were too strong in the circles around princes and governors for it to be possible to moderate the excesses of the tax collectors and to refrain from exploiting the disarmed peasant populations wrongfully. Here, however, it was a question of the defects of the political system rather than the influence of the 'Islamic' mentality properly speaking.

On the other hand, it cannot be disputed that the troubles of periods of war or revolt as well as the slightest changes in the social structure had their repercussions on agricultural conditions and were able to damage its functioning for a long time, thus driving human groups hitherto sedentary to leave their lands. This phenomenon, difficult to reverse, was seen on numerous occasions, and the internal wars witnessed by Iraq in the tenth, eleventh and twelfth centuries resulted in serious damage to the irrigation system which the governors tried in vain to repair; from this there followed a slow but progressive abandonment of lands which went back to their former aridity. Similarly the granting by the 'Abbāsid caliphate to mercenary leaders of foreign origin in ever-increasing numbers of the right to collect the tax on lands previously subjected to tithes or the normal land tax had the disastrous corollary that the oversight was left to temporary masters who took no interest in their upkeep. The system, begun in the Būyid period and developed in the Seljuk period, brought with it a shrinkage of the cultivated areas in so far as the power of a more and more intrusive military caste made itself felt. We find ourselves in the presence of one of those historical phenomena which, properly speaking, it would be wrong to link with the extension of Islam. Historical phenomena emerge again to explain numerous other cases of the appearance of deserts, including the consequences of disastrous invasion mentioned later or, again, this interruption of Mediterranean commerce which brought about, for example, the abandonment of the culture of the olive in the hinterland of Antioch in northern Syria, which became from that moment the 'region of dead towns'.

On the other hand, in order the show the influence of nomadism under Islam, the appearance of nomadic Muslim states from the tenth to the eleventh century is sometimes quoted. But there again, what is the worth of the examples cited? The Carmathians of Bahrein doubtless included in their ranks a large proportion of pillaging bedouin accustomed to the razzia, and this justifies the fear which they spread abroad for many decades in lower Iraq and even in Arabia where they attacked pilgrim caravans: the territory given over to their demands nevertheless always remained limited. Indeed at the same period 'Arab' principalities saw the light of day here and there, such as that of the Mirdasids at Aleppo in the eleventh century, but their strength did not come to them from the role played there by the genuine bedouin. If, from another side, the Fatimids, who seized power in Ifriqiya in 909, were aided by the Kutāma Berbers, in part nomadic, the state which they set up in no way merits the same description. As for the famous Hilal tribe which these same Fatimids, after settling in Egypt, sent into Ifriqiya to punish the recalcitrant Zīrid rulers, they did not for all that found a 'nomadic state' since they were content to repel every form of civilisation in the areas they overran. Indeed, it is only in a recent period that there have appeared states with a bedouin base, notably in Arabia and Transjordan. In the medieval period the phenomenon has not been recorded. All that one notices is that at moments when central power was weak, for example in the tenth and eleventh centuries, the nomads played a greater role, and that then some Arabs of the desert achieved, in limited areas, a certain political autonomy.

4 The invasions

On the other hand, it is certain that non-Arab invasions on a large scale on various occasions at the heart of the Islamic world came to disturb the relations between bedouin and sedentary peoples which had scarcely changed since the period of the first conquests, and also to leave their mark on all medieval Muslim history. These invaders were able to operate all the more easily because the empire's territories covered vast unpopulated, badly defended regions which were thus well-suited for infiltration and raiding by armed bands, especially on the borders of Central Asia and the Sahara, whence came some of the most violent attacks.

As early as the ninth century the 'Abbāsid caliphs had had

occasion to recruit mercenaries; some were Turks or Iranians coming from the frontier regions where they had been reduced to slavery and made prisoners in razzias, some were negroes mostly originating from the Sudan; these former nomads, transplanted into a sedentary environment, came to form distinct social groups which had at times been isolated from the population. The same system was soon practised in Spain where Slavs of white race predominated; and in the same way it enabled the Fātimids to build up powerful armies. But this limited introduction of war-like and half-civilised elements, of different ethnic origins, had nothing in common with what followed later.

Much more laden with consequences was in fact the role played by the Oghuzz who invaded eastern Iran at the beginning of the eleventh century, preceded by Turkish groups who had infiltrated earlier to put themselves at the service of the Muslim governors of Khorasan and who had since then succeeded in preserving their tribal cohesion to the extent of seizing, under their own leaders, whole territories. The Karakhānids, for example, converted in the middle of the tenth century as a result of contact with the Samānids who controlled Transoxiana, had installed themselves in the province as the Samānid power was declining there. They had occupied the region of Bukhara and subsequently extended their territory, where they remained until the beginning of the eighth century, ruling according to their own family customs and dividing up between two principal dynastic lines, in the east and west of Turkestan, a kingdom which was never centralised.

They did not penetrate further into the Empire because they came up against the resistance of the Ghaznavids, rulers who got their name from the city of Ghazna, in Afghanistan, where they had established themselves as independent rulers after having fought as mercenaries in the service of the same Samānids. Turkish in origin, Subuktegin and his descendants, while extending their conquests from Khorasan to Sistan and above all to India, knew how to absorb the governmental and administrative organisation implanted by Islam in these regions. The Ghaznavid state was in fact the first Muslim state arising from deep acculturation of Asian invaders. This was different from the Tulūnid and Ikhshīdid principalities in Egypt which had indeed had at their head Turkish officers although their existence did not depend on the preponderance of groups of this ethnic origin.

The Ghaznavid state opened up the way for the Seljuk state which, too, was a Turkish state dependent on Turkish military forces, but living according to the ancient Iranian and Arabo-Islamic customs. We know that the Seljuks gradually occupied the whole of Iran, pushing back the Ghaznavids eastwards and bringing various towns under their domination, like Nishapur, Rayy, Hamadhan, Isfahan and Shiraz, before reaching Iraq where they put an end to the regime of the 'great emirs' of the Būyid dynasty shortly before the arrival of the Crusaders in Syria. Other bands of Turcomans spread into Azerbayjan and from there into Armenia as well as into the eastern provinces of the Byzantine empire. The sultan Alp Arslan who became the head of a movement at first apparently spontaneous, later won the battle of Manzikert in 1071 against Romanus Diogenes, thus opening Anatolia to the Turks.

This invasion by the Seljuk Turks – so-called because they were descended from a certain Seljuk – had important consequences for the evolution of the Islamic world. Not only was the rough Anatolian territory from now on linked with the commercial routes which had developed there; not only was the so-called Sunni tendency strengthened at the centre of the ancient 'Abbāsid empire; but the social equilibrium was considerably modified by the influx of Turkish elements, essentially military, which merged with the local populations in a proportion which always varied according to the region. It is clearly impossible to reckon the number of these 'invaders'; if one talks of 16,000 men engaged in the battle of Dandanakan against the Ghaznavids, it is possible that we are dealing solely with a first wave and that the flow of Turcomans into Islamic lands continued for long years.

The heads of the Seljuk family, the first 'sultans', however, succeeded for half a century in dominating a vast collection of 'Turkish' principalities stretching from Transoxiana to

Mesopotamia, which were governed, with the help of Iranian administrators, by 'feudal lords' provided with numerous gifts of land. Without doubt some of these leaders had conducted isolated actions frowned on by the central power, like the famous Atsiz who occupied Damascus in 1076 and subsequently had to hand over his position to Tutush, the brother of the Seljuk sultan of the moment. Without doubt, too, the bands which attacked Azerbayjan and then Armenia, do not seem to have obeyed the orders of the 'great sultan': it was only when they reached Byzantine territory that their action was for a moment controlled shortly before the decisive battle that they had to wage; but their spirit of independence was preserved subsequently in Anatolia where internal family feuds only ceased, temporarily, and that with the political rise of the Seljuks of Rum, a collateral branch of the 'great Seljuks'.

But this somewhat anarchical liberty did not prevent the new masters of power from achieving lasting results. Their venture had repercussions on the structure of Muslim society. It assured this society's hold on new geographical areas by islamisation and military occupation, but it equally led to its break-up and diversification by ensuring the pre-eminence, among local non-Arab régimes, of cultural languages which were no longer necessarily and uniquely Arabic.

This Seljuk invasion was soon followed by other movements of the same kind coming from the East. Certainly conquering invasions like those of the Khwarizmians who reached Jerusalem at the beginning of the eighth century, left few traces. But more important and much more devastating was the Mongol invasion of 1258–60 which involved the pillaging and sacking of all the large towns of the eastern Islamic world, in Iran, Iraq, and even in Syria. Only Egypt was spared, thanks to the military resistance of the Mamluks, recently come to power, who stopped the Muslim advance on the borders of Palestine, while the Seljuk princes of Anatolia accepted a sort of protectorate and so spared their country from the worst disasters. In any case it is remarkable that the leaders of these new Asian hordes, not islamised or only superficially islamised in the beginning, also received the mould of the civilisation which they had almost destroyed, so that a little later they formed an authentic Muslim dynasty.

As for the West in this same period, it too did not remain free from invasion. Here it was Berber invasions with smaller numbers that occurred. The Almoravids who conquered the extreme Maghrib, then the whole of the Maghrib, came from the Sahara and the valley of the Niger. Their arrival led to the unification of the Maghrib and of the last, still independent, bastions of a Muslim Spain whose petty kings, mutually divided, maintained themselves with difficulty against the Christians of the reconquest. This had important consequences both for the defence of Islam and for the cultural evolution of Spain and the Maghrib. Somewhat similar was the progress later on of the Almohads, other Berbers who replaced the former and in turn imposed an original régime by force.

Thus this medieval phenomenon of invasions, which each time was provoked in part by the riches of the Muslim countries exposed to the greed of the nomadic barbarians around them, appears as an essential feature in the evolution of the Islamic world and one on which it is right to insist. The historians up till now have been content to consider the stages and progress of the invasions, but to their accounts one may now add the conclusions of those who have endeavoured to underline the irreversibility of the internal changes of all kinds which resulted from such unforeseen influxes. The ruins accumulated on these occasions or brought about by less spectacular migrations, like that of the Arab Hilal tribes in Ifriqiya, had almost always a lasting economic or cultural importance. But other domains could have been affected and the newcomers frequently took part, for example, in doctrinal quarrels; it is enough to mention Nizam al-Mulk, the Iranian vizier of the second and third Seljuk sultans in the East, to think of the support that the Shāfiʻite legal school and, to a certain extent, the Ashʻarite theological doctrine, received from the Seljuks in opposition to the strict traditionalism professed by the caliphs. These are so many effects which combined to transform in depth an empire whose fragile structural equilibrium constantly found itself challenged in the course of centuries, thanks to them.

5 Internal factors of diversification

However, even before the effects of these successive invasions, whether from East or West, manifested themselves, the Islamic world had known the interaction of other powerful factors of diversification in the heart of the first territories occupied and as a function of the geographical or ethnic characters proper to each. As we have seen, regions which were part of the same climatic unit in fact included sometimes limitless steppes, sometimes high mountain chains forming a barrier between fragmented plateaux and valleys fertilised by streams, sometimes alluvial plains reduced in places to narrow coastal strips, sometimes well-watered lands and sometimes irrigated oases of desert and mountain where the conditions of life were not always the same. In addition to former interminglings of population, there came to live there, beside conquering Arabs and native Arameans (both Semitic in language), Turks, Iranians, Copts, Berbers or Andalusians who were not of the same race and whose local traditions of every sort had survived efforts of earlier assimilation. Local particularisms, whose natural origin could only be contested with difficulty even if they got their colour from other exigencies, appeared chiefly in the peripheral provinces and offered a choice terrain for dynastic pretensions. So it was that from the middle and the end of the eighth century, Spain and the Maghrib had become progressively separated from the empire which had recently been taken over by the new 'Abbāsid dynasty, and that in the East also local movements of emancipation had appeared.

Azerbayjan, for example, at the beginning of the ninth century, served as a refuge for the partisans of Bābak, whose attempt was only repressed after many years of difficult military campaigns. A little later it was the general Tāhir who claimed a sort of autonomy in the Khorasan which he governed and which was later entrusted to his descendants. At the end of the century the Samānid governors of Transoxiana, without breaking with the caliphate, formed a quasi-autonomous principality, while the leader of a popular militia, who was a coppersmith, installed himself in Sistan, and the black slaves from lower Iraq, called Zanj, revolted and for several years held in check the caliph's armies. Still later it was the partisans of the movement called Qarmatian (Carmathian) who gave themselves over to brigandry in Syria, then in Iraq, before forming a state in Arabia at Bahrein, from which they led dangerous incursions, sometimes against the seat of the caliph's governor, sometimes against the holy towns of the Hijaz. Then a Shi'ite sect succeeded, thanks to favourable local conditions, in creating a new caliphate, the Fatimid caliphate, which came into being in Ifriqiya in 909, then established itself in Egypt in 969 by relying on groups until then poorly assimilated; while the followers of another Shi'ite movement, the Zaydites, set up principalities in the peripheral mountain regions, one on the edge of the Caspian Sea which did not last, the other in Yemen which was to last, despite various vicissitudes, right down to the present day.

Thus regional peculiarities and sectarian or social movements combined to make the Arab-Islamic world from the tenth to the eleventh centuries a mosaic of principalities or of states with uncertain boundaries which the migrations of the eleventh to twelfth centuries were to come into conflict with and further modify. Each time new dynasties sprang up whose replacement of one another often appears monotonous and of little interest. But we must not lose sight of the fact that such political changes were in part the result of dissensions already present because of the variety of populations involved, and that they themselves brought with them modifications which added further to the complexity of the local contexts in which they developed.

The part played by regional or racial factors in the emergence of a 'separatist' movement or of a revolt is always very difficult to assess. One can indeed carry out detailed research on the ethnic origin of the leaders of these movements. But the documentation at one's disposal does not make this sort of study easy; and if certain names can for example be described without ambiguity as Berber or Iranian, there were also people of non-Arab origin, who at their conversion had adopted Muslim names which concealed their true origin. It is mostly on probabilities that the historian must depend, all the more so since one cannot establish with precision the proportion of non-Arabs participating in this or that armed revolt. Similarly the arguments drawn from the nature of the doctrines professed by this or that group of opponents to the central régime remain weak. Some of their opinions can certainly be identified as being specially widespread in regions where they corresponded to certain traditional tendencies of the inhabitants; but there again the indications obtained hardly permit one to go beyond the level of probabilities; it is necessary to take account of the numerous other elements, social or religious, which can be distinguished in the origin of many of the movements of independence which contributed to the fragmentation of the medieval Islamic world.

6 Production and exchange

These various centrifugal movements alternating with periodic and opposing efforts at reunification did not prevent the world thus stirred up from preserving among other things a striking homogeneity of its capacities for economic production, which went hand in hand with a relative uniformity of the very nature of the products. The quality of the resources coming from the soil and sub-soil was in fact conditioned by the technical level commonly attained in the different Mediterranean and Asian countries to which we have seen that the expansion of the empire was in practice limited. These countries had at their disposal only the harvests of fertile lands (provided they were properly maintained) and also mineral wealth, at least among those minerals which showed themselves most easily accessible.

Cereals were not lacking, notably in Egypt and Syria; rice was cultivated there in the humid regions and provided almost everywhere the basic nourishment. Vegetables were to be had in plenty, especially in Egypt; fruits were varied and plentiful in the different oases in the plains or on the mountain terraces, from the Maghrib to Transoxiana. Stock-breeding was on the other hand confined to that of the camel, and of sheep and goats, with some herds of cattle (chiefly buffalo) in certain provinces.

Industrial cultivation was for its part especially flourishing: sugar cane in Egypt and Syria, cotton and flax in the same countries; plants used in dyeing appeared in various places, so too plants for perfume; olive groves distinguished the countryside in a certain number of lands. As for products which were gathered, these consisted of wood for heating or construction, generally fairly rare, precious woods of teak from Oman, pearls from the Persian Gulf, aromatic resins from Arabia, to which can be added precious stones from Upper Egypt and the Mediterranean as well as the products of quarries and mines. If dressed stone was widespread in Egypt, Syria, Anatolia and Upper Mesopotamia, there was hardly any in Arabia, not much more in Iraq or in Iran where brick was mostly used, either raw or baked. Gold mines existed in Arabia, in Egypt, but especially in Nubia, while silver was found in Iran and Transoxiana. In a general manner of speaking, then, the medieval Islamic world had at its disposal nearly all the products necessary for supporting its inhabitants and their activities; the only things lacking were certain types of wood essential for building boats, the silk that had to be imported from central Asia and, to a certain degree, the gold which was bought in central Africa.

Kept in being at the level of craftsmanship familiar at the period, the industries corresponded to the nature of the primary materials, local or imported, which they worked to transform. Apart from the food industries producing flour, sugar and oil, the most important was the textile industry which used, in Egypt flax as well as cotton and wool, in Syria and Iraq cotton, in Iraq and in Iran the silk which served to make luxury materials and brocades. Then came the leather industry, spread almost everywhere, glass-making, ceramics, the production of perfume, of papyrus, and especially of the paper for which the technique was imported at the end of the eighth century, not to mention that of carpets, mats, and the working of metals, chiefly iron, but also copper, bronze, silver and gold: articles of luxury, even of great luxury, were added to the most essential objects. The picture which thus emerges from data preserved by Arab geographers of the tenth century still lacks the quantitative precision which would greatly enhance their value, but there is sufficient to emphasise the productivity of the provinces which was maintained by various links in the heart of a commercial empire.

In fact, the constitution of this great unit without frontiers had been partly responsible for the development which the smallest craft techniques experienced. Not only was the activity of the workshops stimulated by the fact that complementary products could be easily exchanged, for example, the original dyes from Iran were used by the textile industry in Egypt while Khuzistan imitated certain cloth made in Egypt. But it was above all the growth of the large towns which favoured industrial development while at the same time they competed in attracting towards their markets the products which were imported from the Far East or East Africa, sometimes even from Europe, and passed through Central Asia, Arabia or the Mediterranean countries. The role played by Baghdad in this connection has been sufficiently stressed by the ancient Arab geographers so that it is unnecessary to emphasis it; such a metropolis which covered an area of about 7,000 hectares and far exceeded the other towns, even Fustat and Basra, was important both by the extent of local consumption and the field which it offered for big business. Thus economic prosperity depended closely on the effects of the rapid urbanisation which had characterised the first centuries of Islam and which the opening-up of the commercial routes had itself contributed to bring about.

But, from another standpoint, did this development challenge the principles of Islam which were applied to commercial transactions as well as to other 'social' activities, and did it sometimes encourage the merchants to transgress these principles? Had Islam favoured the growth of economic life or, on the contrary, opposed it? On this point the orientalists do not always agree, chiefly to the extent that they do not all recognise the same influence of Islamic 'law' on current practice.

From a strictly moral point of view it is certain that Islam always showed itself unfavourable to the accumulation of wealth, as appeared in a certain number of verses in the Koran directed against the Meccans and their activities. Certainly the idea of profit (*kasb*), which forms the basis of commercial organisation, rapidly found protagonists among the Hanafi lawyers at the end of the eighth century, thus justifying the activity of the bourgeois merchants who had come to occupy a more important place in the society of their time. We have seen, too, that mercantilism represented a very old Arab tradition and that the reservations formulated in Muhammad's preaching, in a particular historical context, could only with difficulty hinder this progress. But certain problems raised from a legal point of view always remained delicate to handle.

Usury (*ribā*), for example, was formally condemned by the Koran but on the other hand we know that it was very difficult for merchants not to resort to this practice. Thus an author like the celebrated al-Ghazāli (d. 1111), while maintaining the prohibition, recognised that the practice of usury was very common in his time. Similarly the prescriptions of the Law seem in this respect to have been little regarded, whether recourse was had to legal subterfuge – a practice common in the Hanafi school – or whether one simply disregarded them. The one thing that must be noted, doubtless because of a certain Muslim reserve, is that the money-changers and bankers were generally recruited from among the 'people of the Book', that is to say, Jews or Christians. These were indispensable people in a world where bimetallism was the rule and where coins were valued according to their real weight, at least when important payments were being effected; they often succeeded, by lending at interest or gaining contracts for tax-farming, in building up large fortunes for themselves and possibly offering their services to governments suffering from financial difficulties. Thus it was that the caliph al-Muqtadir, at the beginning of the tenth century, had recourse to the famous Jewish money-changers, Pinhas, called by the historians 'money-changers of the court', who had the state treasury at their mercy before it was the turn of the 'farmers' to exercise their pressure on the government.

Islamic law, if opposed to usury, did not, on the other hand, put any obstacle in the way of contracts of association or limited partnership which made it easier for the great merchants to send out large expeditions in quest of valuable merchandise. Contracts of this type, used since a period long before Islam, had been adopted in a way by the jurists, who had restricted themselves to defining the modalities in terms of certain moral requirements. The same applies to the contracts of sale which had been legalised so as to avoid all deception, all fraudulent practice and all risks, the sale having to be realised immediately and the transfer of the object and of the sum of money having to take place simultaneously. For analogous reasons it was foreseen that the rule of offer and demand was strictly observed in the transactions and that the buyer could not become the victim of an abuse on the part of a seller. These were so many elementary legal arrangements of great importance, which were in general respected, sometimes under the control of a magistrate, the *muhtasib*, also called the inspector of the market, and specially charged with this task among other aspects of his function of *hisba*. At the same time, there were levied on the merchants certain taxes which had not been provided for in the Law but which seem to have been instituted very soon, since they are recorded as early as the seventh century and in the period of the Umayyad caliphs.

Indeed the origins of a market organisation, itself still insufficiently known, remain obscure because of the absence or rarity of texts. We know, thanks to the Arab geographers of the ninth century, that in the large towns of Iraq founded under Islam, the artisans were grouped according to their specialisation and we find the same arrangement in all medieval Islamic cities, whether old or new, with this one exception that the important conurbations added, to their main commercial quarter, suburbs which themselves possessed markets on a smaller scale but always organised on the same principle. Had this arrangement been inherited from antiquity or was it born as the result of new demands? We do not know. One thing is certain, that the Umayyad caliphs developed, in certain towns, specialised markets for the sale of certain objects and that the principle was later universally adopted, whether it was in Iran, the Near East or the Maghrib, for this organisation made it easier to operate controls.

A similar control, which had apparently existed in the 'caravan cities' of Arabia or of the Syro-Mesopotamian desert at an earlier date, had thus been preserved under Islam and integrated, after a fashion, into its ethical system. It would explain the appearance, at a date still impossible to fix, of the function of *hisba* which is, in principle, of a religious and moral character; to this was attached, apart from the task of hunting heresy, the obligation to exercise technical controls such as that of the weights and measures used in commercial transactions. Control of markets, surveillance of morals and repression of heresy were united in this *hisba* to which one is tempted to attribute a pre-Islamic origin. This is what the hypotheses would lead us to think which have best emphasised the background, finding in it, besides the function of the agoranomos in the Byzantine towns, various other precedents recorded in the towns of the ancient East. In this domain as in others, the pre-existing practice, adopted to the extent that it did not contradict the principles of Islam, had left a mark on the moral and economic order to which Islam had given birth by virtue of a process to which we shall return later.

But the economic development as such was equally conditioned by the tax system operating in the empire, a tax system which also rested in part on former customs. We have already seen that a high tax hit the native inhabitants of the countries, varying according to the quality of the cultivation, and that it had an effect prejudicial to agricultural development. The taxes levied on the merchants and justified by the jurists in an indirect manner were equally inspired by ancient models, even if the tax system favoured the Muslims, as far as big business went, to the detriment of dependent non-Muslims and foreigners. We also know that this development profited from the banking practices used by Islam for the transfer of funds, such as the different forms of letters of credit. However, we know little about the manner in which these business operations were carried out because we lack archival documents; the large collection of documents known by the name of Geniza which was found in a Cairo synagogue, remains of marginal value as it deals essentially with the Jewish population. For their part, the information from ancient Arab sources, for example, the strange tales of the geographer Ibn Khurdadhbih in the ninth century concerning on one hand the Russian merchants, on the other the 'radanite' Jewish merchants who came from the Frankish countries, remain difficult to interpret because they consist of itineraries full of contradictions and perhaps valid for a much earlier period. All we get is the impression that, in forms which are partly unknown to us, the Muslim world was in regular contact with the Slav world, the Byzantine world, central Asia, the Far East and the Christian West.

On this last point the consequences of economic development of the medieval Islamic world have given rise to controversies. It has been maintained – this is Henri Pirenne's famous thesis – that the ending of trade with Europe, or at least its notable diminution, had driven the latter to turn to an economy based on the land. This thesis remains much disputed in view of the imprecision of the phenomena in question. What we can be sure about is that the domination of Islam over the Mediterranean effectively brought about a distinct lessening of trade in this region, and the evidence that we have on the other hand of the maintenance during the same period of relations between East and West does not invalidate this statement. The fact, however, has hardly been able to explain by itself the economic evolution of the countries of the West, and in this respect more profound research is needed.

On the other hand, for the relations with the Slavonic and Scandinavian countries, we possess important evidence in the form of numerous hoards of Muslim coins found in these countries. They prove the intensity of the trade which occurred during a period which did not go beyond the eleventh century to judge from the date of the coins preserved. The hoards also prove that the silver which came from Muslim countries was used in regions lacking this metal where crafts and commercial development still remained weak. We are on the other hand much less informed on relations with central Asia, from which came Turkish slaves as well as silk, and we do not know much more about the Far East. Various travellers' tales certainly show us that Muslim navigators ventured much further eastwards, but we have not been given any concrete data.

It is moreover evident that the great trade routes commonly used in the interior of the Islamic world experienced throughout the Middle Ages variations which for some were important. Of these variations, linked in general to a political situation which was a response to the economic development, the most notable was the transfer of big business from Baghdad to Cairo, which took place when the Fatimid caliphate established itself in Egypt and extended its domination to Syria. It was through the Red Sea and not through the Arab-Persian Gulf that the ships which carried on trade with Southern Arabia and the Far East passed, and it was to Cairo, too, or to Alexandria, that the European merchants came to buy the goods that interested them. Parallel to this transfer, Baghdad, which had fallen to the rank of provincial capital, although it was still the seat of the 'Abbāsid caliphate, was then cut off from its Mediterranean outlets. A little later still, after the occupation of Anatolia by the Turks, a new route from Tabriz gained the Asiatic trade from the north, confirming Baghdad's decline but also leading to that of Egyptian commerce. It would be necessary likewise to bring in the changes experienced by trade on the 'silk road' in terms of the possibilities of travelling to the heart of Asia, and to take account of the situation in the Maghrib where several trade routes from east to west were followed according to the period. The last of these, the coastal route, was the most difficult to develop because of natural obstacles and despite the existence of important towns on its itinerary.

Much research will still be necessary in order to retrace the history of these commercial links. It will mean having to use at one and the same time information from books, which is generally too succinct, and archaeological evidence, which is unequal and dispersed, about the stages and caravanserais which lined the routes. But it also demands a rigorous observing of chronology to allow us to follow a reality much more fluid than any one up to now has wanted to admit. This means that the conclusions in this field remain, and are likely to remain for long, incomplete.

None the less the fact remains that it cannot be denied that intense commercial activity had always existed across the vast ancient Islamic world and this was the case whatever dynasties were set up here and there and also whatever routes were followed. Few fundamental economic transformations seem in fact to have occurred during the Middle Ages, whose repercussions on political and social evolution can be seen; rather it was the opposite which occurred to judge by the changes of route which were brought about here and there by the chances of historical conjunction. Such a rigidity, too, of the conditions of business and production, at least until the middle of the thirteenth century, could have caused a comparable rigidity of prices also. Recent researches undertaken on this subject would tend at least to make one believe this, even if the studies are still in their early stages through lack of sufficient data from the sources or through lack of conclusions obtained from monetary history, which at the moment has barely been outlined. This general impression, then, gives authority only to indicate in passing one of the very interesting questions which is open to future investigations and from which one may expect a new understanding of the realities of daily life at the heart of medieval Islam.

CHAPTER 3
Aspects of Islamic doctrine

All too often Islamic doctrine is thought of as a relatively simple collection of beliefs, moral principles, social rules and rituals which sufficed to give the corresponding civilisation the unity so often highlighted: in fact, adherence to the Muslim religion is expressed by pronouncing a short formula, the 'profession of faith' (*shahāda*) which on the one hand affirms divine uniqueness and on the other recognises Muhammad's mission. This basic faith is nevertheless accompanied by a number of other ideas, developed in the course of the centuries along varied lines of reflection. The result is that in reality it presents different aspects which correspond not only to the disciplines whose influence more or less determined its development in each period but also to the currents of thought whose vitality expressed itself historically by struggles and more or less heated discussions.

These aspects have not ceased to pose problems for students of Islam who have taken up divergent positions on the evolution of the doctrine they studied, very often as divergent as their reactions towards Islam as a religion, since some of them were thus led to favour the current of thought with which they found themselves personally in harmony. As for the historians properly speaking, they have been above all preoccupied with the repercussions which the doctrinal development had on the political and social transformations of the Islamic world in the course of its long history.

Indeed, the first important point is to connect the different aspects of the doctrine with the very nature of the Koranic message which supports them, beginning with data at once religious and juridical. Religious data were present because, while defining new rules about worship, this message set out beliefs destined to replace Arab paganism and to be substitutes for those hitherto proclaimed by the other monotheistic religions. Juridical data were present because they established fundamental rules for public and private life around which the new community was organised.

I The elaboration of 'law' and the science of the 'traditions'

Such a message, outlining the main directions of a religion concerned with the temporal as much as with the spiritual order, demanded gradual definition on many points; during Muhammad's life-time the attitude of the Prophet himself made this possible. The Koranic injunctions thus found themselves completed by what was called the custom or *sunna* of the Prophet and this was later extended by the living tradition of the community. Other difficulties were raised, from the first centuries, over the vast area conquered by Islam, and as a result of the contacts there established with the defenders of earlier doctrines; these difficulties had often to be regulated by means other than simple recourse to the Prophet's example and that of his first Companions. This was done in the climate of somewhat disorganised improvisations which the community experienced soon after Muhammad's death.

Once the Prophet had gone, the era of 'prophecy' had in fact been thought of as ended and only certain extremists from the Shi'ite sects still believed that the divine will would continue to manifest itself to guide them. For the others, the Revelation given once for all, would never continue in the same conditions. From now on, all that remained was to interpret and apply the different provisions which it contained. But the Prophet's successors who, to a certain extent, were his 'heirs', only held limited powers to do this, very different from those Muhammad had exercised during his lifetime as transmitter of the Word of God itself.

Admittedly the first caliphs were compelled to set up some arrangements of a practical nature not expressly provided for by the letter of the Koran, for example, in connection with the law of inheritance or certain supererogatory prayers. As we have seen, they had also to set up a fiscal system corresponding to the new situation created by the extension of the conquests: the simple system followed until then did not suit the land tenure of the occupied provinces and it fell to the Umayyad caliphs to make rules for a new land tax. But other areas eluded them longer. Thus penal justice was the concern of cadis who were closely dependent (in the early days at least) on the local governors and who did not always strictly follow the letter of Revelation. It seems that there was hesitation in cutting off the hand of a thief and that, in legal proceedings, the judges attached to oral evidence an importance that was not justified by the Koran; the application of the law, generally speaking, was established empirically and often rested on old customs as much as on the recommendations of the Prophet. This was an anarchical situation due to the relative freedom allowed to each judge, or, in important matters, to each governor; the practice was particularly denounced in the middle of the eighth century by Ibn al-Muqaffa'. This author and original thinker, passing himself off as counsellor to the prince, advised the 'Abbāsid caliph al-Mansūr to take decisions himself which, once gathered together in a sort of legal code, would gain respect in the empire as a whole.

In fact, Ibn al-Muqaffa' was not followed, and it reverted to isolated jurists, reacting against this 'Umayyad practice' which was hesitant and badly co-ordinated, to define the principles which would have to be followed in order to resolve concrete problems. Among them in this eighth-century environment were Mālik (d. 793) working in Medina and Abū Hanīfa (d. 767) working in Mesopotamia, both of whom showed disapproval of 'Abbāsid power. Their words and those of their followers formed the doctrinal basis of the two schools known as Mālikite and Hanafite which were later reckoned among the official Sunnite schools of law. Both made use of what is called 'personal reflection' (*ijtihād*) but profited from it to establish genuine rules for the elaboration of Islamic law. The first, Mālik, aimed at upholding the principle of the common good (*maslaha*) which served to guide jurists in cases of litigation; the other, Abū Hanīfa, defended the principle called *istihsān* which consisted in choosing the 'best' solution. Only from this moment did the Law begin to take shape: solutions were put forward for the different cases which came up and these solutions were drawn together in collections which constituted the first law treatises. The oldest was the *Muwattā*, 'the well-trodden', by Mālik, which was followed by writings compiled by the disciples of Abū Hanīfa, such as the famous al-Shaybani.

But the positions of these first doctors provoked in turn reactions from other jurists who thought that the principles adopted by Mālik and Abū Hanīfa lacked force. Thus al-Shāfi'i (d. 820) claimed to return to the 'traditions' of the Prophet, that is, to his sayings and deeds, in order to settle all lawsuits, only accepting recourse to 'reasoning by analogy' (*qiyās*) in cases where the traditions were unable to provide the necessary elements. As for Ibn Hanbal (d. 855) he wanted to follow even more strictly the ancient practice of the community; this is why he was one of the first to make a collection of the 'traditions' or *hadīths* to which the jurists looked for guidance when taking decisions. To determine the value of these different *hadīths* he attributed such importance to the authorities who vouched for them, that he classed them according to the authorities and not in logical order, thus favouring the development of a science which became absolutely necessary for jurists to cultivate and which consequently experienced a growing development.

The four legal schools thus founded successively by Mālik, Abū Hanīfa, al-Shāfi'i and Ibn Hanbal ended up by being considered as the only schools to which a believer might adhere; this sufficiently explains the role that they played in the lives of Muslims. The principal acts of each individual, whether ritual acts or acts of daily life, were judged by the scale of values set up by the heads of these schools: and further the methods of reasoning used in each group came directly from the thinking of these same heads. It was not Greek logic nor even a substitute for this logic which guided the average believer, but either 'reasoning by analogy' of which the principles still remained vague, or else the preoccupation with public utility or some other consideration going back to the methods of the founder of his school. Thus, despite the relative independence of spirit shown by the jurists who, each in turn, set about examining the 'sources of the law', the authority of the first heads and their immediate followers did not cease to influence the behaviour and mentality of Muslims who later always tried to place themselves in relation to the particular categories of 'law' thus defined.

Moreover it did not seem right to consider this law, as is sometimes done, as a theoretical law far removed from reality; even if its prescriptions were not always observed, even if 'subterfuges' permitted escape from some of its prohibitions, such as that of usury, it preserved the value of a code proposing an ideal to be realised. Still more, the religious man was recognisable in the medieval setting by the fact that he rigorously observed the obligations, even the most onerous; and, because this law distinguished in particular between obligatory acts and 'recommended' acts, between forbidden acts and 'reprehensible' acts, there was an imperceptible transition from Law to ethics.

But the differences between recognised schools of law were not without their repercussions in other domains besides that of the proper legal, moral, and liturgical sphere. Each of these schools had its own particular way of understanding the religious life, a way of reasoning which often recurred in the theological even mystical, doctrines, which will be discussed later. Belonging to one of them generally implied being rooted in one of the movements of thought which divided the medieval Muslim world. Thus the Hanbalites were traditionalists in theology just as they were strict in morals; the Shāfi'ites who admitted reasoning by analogy also admitted certain relationships between God and his creatures and adopted a more flexible theology, while showing their sympathy for mysticism; the Hanafites, on the other hand, who showed themselves to be more independent, willingly cultivated the 'subterfuges' and often sided with a rationalising theology.

We must never forget that these categories of modes of thought had at first nothing restricting about them, and that until the eleventh and twelfth centuries, other juridical schools than the four Sunnite schools already mentioned, had one after the other come into being; they had responded to the efforts of a Syrian such as al-Awzā'i who had undertaken to codify Islamic law in the Umayyad period, as well as jurists from Iraq such as al-Thawri, Abū Dāwūd, the founder of the Zāhirite school, and al-Tabari. The renown temporarily enjoyed by one or other of these schools is sufficient witness to the fact that Islamic law was elaborated slowly and not without contradiction. Indeed it was only in the twelfth century that this appeared with definite contours under the four aspects which were alone authorised at that time and which have remained classic ever since.

Previously, the stages by which this 'elaboration' was reached raised questions which the orientalists have not ceased to discuss among themselves. The principal thing remains to know whether the Law as it is presented today by relatively late treatises, has not been marked by the incorporation of foreign elements and whether the principles of 'personal reflection', which have played a part in most cases, were not, in certain measure, inspired by ways of reasoning employed in other civilisations. It would be the specific character of Islamic law as such which certain observations of this kind would tend to query.

Thus we have noticed how the fiscal organisation which appeared in the Umayyad period had difficulty in claiming that it was following Koranic principles. The land-tax of the tithe to which land-owning Muslims had been subjected had not been provided as such by the sacred text, even if it had been determined by the requirements of the legal alms or *zakāt*. For its part, the rule set out for recent converts had no direct relationship to Koranic precepts but was even contrary to these precepts since the new Muslims saw themselves constrained to pay a tax very much in excess of that paid by the older Muslims. It was the result of pressing government needs which had prevented the Umayyad caliphs from reducing the tax as would have been appropriate on the *mawālī* adhering to Islam and this result had been obtained by deciding that the land tax or *kharāj* would be based on landed property whatever the religion of its occupant. The system was certainly justified juridically by the assimilation of the 'conquered' lands to booty which became the property of the community and by identification of the new tax with a 'rent'. But although the principles were safe, the arrangements thus adopted stemmed much more from dispositions prior to Islam than from the preaching of Muhammad and they were a long way from respecting the principle of equality needed among Muslims.

Even the practice of *waqf* or 'mortmain', which appeared very soon, apparently came into being through the working together of different factors. If *waqf* could be justified by the recommendation that the Prophet had made to his Companions to contribute to the cost of the legal war, it is also seen to be so close to the types of pious foundations used by the oriental Christian churches that it is difficult not to see there an influence of the surrounding milieu. If we also consider the fact that it was practised by certain Muslims in order to get round the rules of inheritance, it seems impossible that in its final form it had been shaped by the effect of Koranic injunctions alone. We find again in this case a situation similar to that which has allowed us to recognise, in the elaboration of certain contracts of rent or sale, the use of concepts very near to those of Roman law and due without doubt to the experience of the new converts.

Certainly the reality of the influences thus admitted remains difficult to demonstrate, and it is difficult to dismiss the hypothesis that, in similar circumstances, different social groups might themselves have been able to reach comparable conclusions. But the length of time which was necessary for a relative codification of the Law, the number of the *mawālī* who participated in this work, and the place accorded by the most eminent jurists to customary law when it did not contradict the prescriptions of the Koran, made it easy to believe that foreign materials were incorporated in the course of this codification. The science of the principles or 'roots' of law (*usūl al-fiqh*) in particular had appealed to all sorts of maxims and principles, each of which authorised different approaches, but the study of these has not yet reached a satisfactory conclusion.

Whatever the position here, the law thus appeared as a separate branch of the religious sciences employing a special technique which is seen to become progressively more specific over the centuries. But as we have seen, it nevertheless remained closely bound, among these same sciences, to theology, and above all, to the science of the traditions on which it depended, though it also encouraged the development of this.

In fact we know that, from the beginning of Islam, the words of the Prophet as well as the stories relating to his acts and deeds had been collected and transmitted. These 'traditions', which were a justification for the different decisions taken by the leaders of the first Islamic community as well as for the doctrines they professed, were used at one and the same time in matters of law, politics and theology. However, it was above all the attitude of the head of the juridical school, such as al-Shāfi'i and Ibn Hanbal, which led the Muslims to gather together those traditions whose authenticity it seemed possible to establish and to distinguish them from the different and sometimes contradictory traditions which had seen the light in the course of the first two centuries.

The science of the traditions, the rules for which were formulated in the ninth century to allow the formation of the first great collections of *hadīths*, was based essentially on the examination of 'chains' of guarantors which preceded each of the transmitted traditions. A tradition was considered to be authentic if the different authorities named were themselves worthy of confidence and if, in addition, the chain of guarantors showed no gap, that is to say, if each of the persons mentioned, given their respective ages, could effectively have transmitted the tradition in question to his successor in the chain.

But the method adopted by the Muslims of this period to identify, from purely external criteria, the 'prophetic traditions' on which they relied would not satisfy those contemporary students of Islam who in the name of modern science, want more rigorous results, while new perspectives for the treatment of data of this kind are now opened up by recourse to computer science. The analysis of the contents of the traditions themselves would be desirable but nothing is more difficult than to try to assess their value. Certainly one can in many cases see the link which existed between a particular *hadīth* and the juridical and theological position which it seemed to justify. This followed a process practised by all those who participated in the activity of doctrinal reflection which characterised the first centuries of Islam, as well as by all those who later defended the more or less deviationist sectarian movements to which they had adhered. But when the historian tries to determine in more precise manner the detail of the interventions and misrepresentations, he is obliged to recognise his powerlessness and content himself by picking out the signs which lead him to a reasonable interpretation without providing him with any certainty.

Take some significant examples. When the Prophet declares, in his farewell speech, that all, Arabs and non-Arabs, are equal, must one believe that this 'saying' is authentic? It is noticeable that only relatively late authors report a saying whose importance we have already underlined above, and that they do so precisely at the period when the struggles for influence between Arabs and non-Arabs were acute; this observation militates rather in favour of the 'insertion' of such a saying after the event in the original text of the discourse, but that is as far as one can go. Similarly if one observes the different roles attributed, in the biographers of the Prophet, to his uncle al-'Abbās, who, according to the version, joined the new religion after a shorter or longer delay, one could not fail to connect these differences with the claims of the 'Abbāsid rulers. These were the descendents of al-'Abbās who seized power in Iraq in 750 and who made a point of underlining the important place that their ancestor had occupied in the spread of Islam. This makes room for doubts about the formulations most favourable to al-'Abbās but, properly speaking, proves nothing. Similarly again, even when we find ourselves confronted with a series of traditions condemning the usage of reasoning by analogy, we are led to see there assertions brought together by the adversaries of the Shāfi'ite school; but it would be rash to pass final judgment on the authenticity of the stories concerned.

2 The first theological discussions

If it is then necessary to consider, with some caution, traditions corresponding to a well-defined political or juridical tendency, but difficult to reach assured results, the process becomes even more delicate when one comes to the realm of theology where those arguing likewise had recourse to the authority of the Prophet. The discussions about the theology began in fact early on, even if they did not lead immediately to the composition of treatises, and they too depended, perhaps even more than the controversies of juridical character, on political questions. Such questions had a practical bearing because in Islam the role played by theology was not, as in Christianity, to illuminate certain points of dogma, but to make it possible either to take sides in favour of the legitimacy of such or such a power, or to reply to criticisms formulated by non-Muslims. Rough outlines of reflection of this sort made their appearance in order to defend partisan attitudes or to refute criticisms, which employed traditions which could have been forged for immediate needs, though nothing is indicated with certainty.

In any case, the first theological subjects discussed are known to us; they concerned the imāmate and the conditions requisite for exercising the function of imam. It was a question of defending claims aimed at restoring the rights of 'Ali, the son-in-law and cousin of the Prophet, against those of the first caliphs who had risen to power before him. Thus arose two doctrines, the one called Shi'ite from the name of the party (*shī'a*) of 'Ali, and the other Khārijite from the name of the followers of 'Ali who revolted against him after having at first supported him. But what must be stressed is that the discussions begun in this spirit had a bearing not only on the qualities of the authority recognised in everyone invested with the imamate, but also on other more common subjects which appeared during the course of events. When for example the battle took place between 'Ali and his opponents, Talha and al-Zubayr, supported by 'Āisha, the Prophet's widow, a fight which received the name of 'the battle of the camel', the Muslims immediately asked themselves who among the believers was guilty of having taken up arms against other believers: the followers of 'Ali accuse his enemies; the enemies of 'Ali threw the responsibility back on him, and considered all the accused as excluded from the community for having committed 'a grave fault', namely, that of having spilt blood.

Some later asked themselves if such an attitude – whoever was responsible for it – was really a grave fault demanding repentance and which, if not followed by repentance, condemned its perpetrator to hell. Others were tempted not to take sides in this quarrel and to remain neutral, while maintaining that one of the two groups was at fault. It is the problem of faith (*īmān*) or, more exactly, of the status of the believer, which is thus raised. What was necessary for the believer in order to be and to remain a member of the community? Was it sufficient to adhere to the simple articles of faith? Was it further necessary to maintain a strict observance of the prescriptions of the Law leading one to behave outwardly as a model Muslim?

The status of the believer was thus at first discussed in the context of a war-like confrontation and it continued to be discussed with bitterness because the legitimacy of the reigning caliphs was not at stake. It was admitted that the caliph must necessarily possess the quality of believer; but did he lose this quality and become unworthy of this function if he committed an offence, a lapse, or a simple injustice? The Umayyad caliphs sought to demand an unconditional obedience and for this reason encouraged the doctors of the Murji'ite persuasion who held that one should not pass judgment here below on the behaviour of believers; thus, according to them, anyone who affirmed his faith in Islam was a believer and remained a believer. The opposite view was held by the Khārijites whose doctrine took shape after the battle of Siffin in 657 between 'Ali and Mu'āwiya, but who represented an older line of thought, demanding strict respect for the Law: whoever departed from this line of conduct was put out of the community and considered an infidel (*kāfir*), if not physically eliminated; in consequence the caliph, like any other believer, had to submit himself to the judgment of the Muslims as a whole since they were in a way the guardians of the truth.

This problem of 'faith' and of the definition of the believer was not always the only problem discussed from an early period. That of free will was another, in conditions which are still vague and which have been the object of different opinions; there is indeed ground for asking whether influences foreign to Islam did not impinge on this subject on which the Koranic text lacks precision. Numerous passages speak of the Judgment which men will undergo in the Hereafter, a judgment in the course of which they will be rewarded or punished according to the deeds they have accomplished here below and for which they will be held responsible; but there are other verses which appear to take away from man, mere creature, all volition and personal responsibility. Is it not stated for example, that God 'misleads whom he will' and 'guides in the right way whom he will'? In Islam, even more than in Christianity, since the reconciling of free will and divine omnipotence is not always easy to achieve, it is found that numerous traditions insist that God is both omnipotent and arbitrary, thus leaving man with very little freedom. Thus everything points to the belief that the early caliphs, especially the Umayyads, favoured the belief in divine 'constraint' as it was then called. To reduce the responsibility of the individual was also to restrict the responsibility of the ruler who henceforward was no longer accountable to his subjects. Jabrism (from the word *jabr* – 'constraint') had just reinforced Murji'ism to impose a total obedience to the imām in power.

Nevertheless, Umayyad rule, for reasons which we do not need to examine here, did not escape being criticised, often with violence. The caliphs were accused of impiety by the Medinan circles who blamed them for getting too involved in questions of government and of losing sight of the demands of the Koranic message; they were treated as usurpers by the Shi'ites and further, in Syria and Iraq, they were the target for attacks by opposing elements of whom some devoted themselves to revolutionary activities. If al-Hasan al-Basri, author of a letter addressed to the caliph 'Abd al-Mālik about 695, remained on the level of doctrine and tried to show that God cannot be responsible for the evil committed by man, nor in a general way for the evil existing in the world, other individuals embarked on open warfare against the caliphs, whose dismissal they demanded because of their bad conduct. Such was the attitude of Ma'bad al-Juhani who was in fact a friend of al-Hasan al-Basri. A little later, in the caliphate of Hishām, a certain Ghaylān, a finance officer of Coptic origin, rebelled in no uncertain manner against the régime of whose direction he disapproved, while maintaining a doctrine fairly close to Khārijite ideas. He was executed, and a little later, Yazīd III who had come to the throne as the result of insurrection, officially approved his doctrines, which were at one and the same time religious and political, and according to which the caliph had to be held responsible for his acts. The same ruler strove to establish strict equality between Arabs and non Arab converts, because the policy of assimilation or non-assimilation of the latter constituted at that time a stumbling-block for the régime: it was the rejection of this assimilation, openly professed by the successors of the caliph 'Umar II, which had provoked the hostility of the new Muslims and led them, in consequence, to adopt the contrary opinion to that of the Jabrites. This is called Qadarite because it consisted in restricting the omnipotence (*qadar*) of God so as to reassert the value of human activity.

The individuals who supported this Qadarite doctrine, still expressed in a confused way and according to slightly different formulations, were sometimes of Christian origin. Now we know that the Christian theologians of the time were asking themselves exactly similar questions to those which, on the theoretical plane, were disturbing Muslim thinkers; they were asking themselves, for example, if God, who could not be considered as the cause of adultery, is the creator of a child born of adultery. From that, some have been tempted to conclude that Christian questioning had an influence on Muslim reflection about the freedom of the will, since it would be impossible to affirm that the origins of such reflection were purely political. Other orientalists, however, have maintained that such a meeting between Muslim and Christian thought was purely accidental and that the Qadarite movement had developed according to its own logic. But we must not forget that from the Umayyad period, Christian authors had taken it upon themselves to refute Islam by criticising, in particular, belief in 'predestination', which was currently widespread among the Muslims and which the rulers had doubtless helped to spread. Their attitude tended to encourage the thought that the converts who defended Qadarite theses had remained imbued with their former convictions.

On the other hand, from the end of the Umayyad period it seems that discussion had begun about the idea of God and especially of the nature of the Koran as the 'Word of God'. The question is particularly obscure because since the real controversies on this subject took place a century later, it is always possible to ask if the information concerning the first protagonists of the thesis of the 'created Koran' had not been forged so as to place, at an earlier date, the arguments put forward at the beginning of the ninth century: each side had really wanted to make its standpoint as strong as possible. Certain signs make one tend to think that the person to whom is attributed the doctrine of the created Koran, Ja'd ibn Dirham, who lived at the beginning of the eighth century and was executed by the Umayyad governor Khālid al-Qasri about 743, had really defended this doctrine which was later adopted by others. A certain Jahm, who participated actively in an anti-Umayyad revolt in eastern Iran and who was captured and executed in 746, also professed, it is said, a body of dubious opinions among which featured the belief in the created Koran. Certain data, very slender for all that, would have us believe that in his case even the idea of God was in dispute, since he declared that God could not have spoken to Moses, contrary to what is written in the Koran following Biblical tradition, and that God could not have had Abraham for 'friend'. Could not there have been some influence of the ancient philosophers whose works had begun to be translated into Arabic at the end of the Umayyad period and which were already known to the Christian communities who had Syriac translations of them? In this way one could explain that the doctrine of this mysterious Jahm came into being as a reaction to anthropomorphism.

In this desire for greater theological depth, an attempt has also been made to see a reply to accusations coming from Christians. The Christians were in fact led to ask the Muslims about the nature of the Word of God, which was identified in a Koranic verse with the humanity of Christ, although more generally the phrase designated the text of the Koran itself. The Muslims in replying to this question found themselves, according to their reply, either obliged to recognise the divinity of Christ, which was contrary to their basic doctrine, or instead led to acknowledge the created character of the Koran. It is certain that such considerations came into play at some time, but they probably did so at a later date, and in the end there is nothing to prove that they were at the origin of the opinions of Ja'd or Jahm.

On the other hand, such persons were clearly enemies of the Umayyads, and their doctrines were doubtless linked in part with their political attitude. Thus Jahm seems to have wanted to criticise a régime accused of laxity, while for his part maintaining a strict respect for the Book of God and the *sunna*, accompanied by elements such as the idea of the 'created Koran'. As for Ja'd, whose attitude is less clear, it could be that his only crime was to want to 'reason' about questions of dogma and to challenge in particular the letter of the Koranic text, thus destroying the edifice on which the authority of the Umayyad rulers rested. The appearance of this desire to 'reason' remains anyway still unexplained, certainly in our present state of knowledge.

3 The Mu'tazilite theses

After the accession of the 'Abbāsid caliphs in 750, there appeared a genuine theological school which was given the name 'Mu'tazilite' by its adversaries. Its first representatives, two *mawālī* named Wāsil and 'Amr, had not, it seems, up to this moment elaborated a complete and coherent doctrine. Nevertheless they had already made themselves felt on the political as well as on the religious level and the movement to which they belonged had perhaps gone so far as to support the 'Abbāsid party. This last hypothesis certainly lacks proof and does not seem to be confirmed by the direction taken later by the new caliphate.

The first Mu'tazilite movement, whose origin seems to go back a long way in the history of the Islamic community, remains in fact very vague in outline. The historians merely remark the existence of groups or isolated individuals who practised *i'tizāl*, that is to say, 'withdrawal', or as we would say, neutralism, at the time of the various confrontations which had developed in the community. Such an attitude could be both political and spiritual or intellectual, but, according to the reports of the heresiographers, the political aspect had always predominated in the emergence of Mu'tazilism. One of the main ideas attributed to Wāsil was in fact that one ought not to pass judgment on believers who had fought against one another and of whom certain had been in error although one could not recognise with certainty on which side the faults were. Wāsil, thus refraining from taking sides, joined neither the camp of 'Ali's followers nor that of his opponents, and, among others, did not accept the condemnations without appeal which the Khārijites had thrown at 'Ali after having at first supported him.

This first idea was accompanied by a second, which, according to some anecdotes, could have been responsible for the name which was given to the followers of Wāsil and which was illustrated by the doctrine, soon to be famous, of the 'intermediate state' of the sinner. This latter was said to have been formulated in the course of a discussion presided over by the ascetic al-Hasan al-Basri where Wāsil is said to have refused to choose between the positions of the Murji'-ites who maintained that the person guilty of a grievous fault was still a believer, and that of the Khārijites who, on the contrary, treated the sinner as an 'infidel' and excluded him from the community. Keeping aloof from the positions of the two opposing groups, Wāsil is said to have declared that such a believer remained in an intermediate state in so far as he had not repented, and his opinion appeared as the transposition to the theological level of the political attitude previously mentioned.

To this fundamental idea two other doctrines were added, one concerning freedom of the will, which was shared, we are told, by 'Amr ibn Ubayd, the other dealing with the attributes of God and the nature of the Koran. These last bore the mark of an intellectualist tendency since they adopted an idea of God which insisted exclusively on His justice, His oneness, and His transcendence, while denying Him all arbitrary initiative. Thus the God on whom the first Mu'tazilites reflected was no longer an omnipotent God whom they had to fear, but a perfectly just and reasonable God whom they had to revere without needing to intercede with Him since He necessarily acted in accordance with what was just.

Such an interpretation in intellectual terms of the religious life was not for all that the work of a group of men imbued with philosophy. It was to be found equally among sectarians as violent as the Khārijites of whose excessive strictness, moreover, the Mu'tazilites did not approve. Rather it betrayed the concern, then shared by various groups of believers, to be faithful to the aspect of the Islamic religion which they considered essential, to the detriment of other aspects judged by them to be secondary. This is to indicate the complexity of the factors present in the formation of Mu'tazilite thought, which had undeniable affinities with Khārijite thought, although this is not sufficiently discussed. It is also to indicate the need in which we stand, in order to deal with problems of this kind, to take account of the political and social context in which they arise without forgetting the influences, perhaps diffuse, which they received from the philosophical thought of antiquity.

The ninth century saw a more precise formulation of doctrine by the great thinkers who gave it a philosophical dimension and who, on the other hand, became well known, thanks to the support of the caliph al-Ma'mūn. The different views ascribed to them by later heresiographers, who attribute several statements to various authors whose works are now lost, did not prevent Mu'tazilism, which had become the doctrine of unity and justice (*al-tawhīd wa-l-'adl*), from presenting itself henceforth in a coherent manner. Its conception of divine unity implied a theodicy insisting on the timeless character of the divinity: God is outside of time, eternal, and outside of space; He is beyond all human categories, is neither substance nor accident, is not begotten, and has not begotten. Such a definition of God, completely negative and closely linked with the Koranic verses of sura 112, 'sincerity', is expressed in terms obviously borrowed from the language of the ancient philosophers, and this proves that the thinking on which the Mu'tazilite scholars relied, in order to clarify fundamental points of dogma, had for its basis processes of reasoning of long standing. The idea of God, One and Transcendent, which was equally opposed to traditional opinions, by leaving little room for 'mercy', further implied important consequences, such as the negation of the divine 'attributes', that is, these qualifications of power, knowledge, life and word (or speech) used by someone when speaking of God.

What was at issue was chiefly a problem of language, but one which released heated discussions in Muslim circles. The Koranic verses proclaim indeed that God is powerful, knowing, living, speaking, that He is 'hearing', 'seeing'; from this it was concluded that God possessed the qualities corresponding to these adjectives. But for the Mu'tazilites this was a position which respected neither the divine unity nor the divine transcendence, for on the one hand, these qualifications could not be at once distinct from God and eternal; on the other hand, it was disturbing to apply them to God when they were appropriate only to creatures, and established similarities or at least analogies between God and the created world in contradiction to other Koranic verses, such as that which asserts 'nothing is similar to Him'.

The Mu'tazilites were thus led to maintain that God has no attribute and that, if He is 'knowing', which they themselves never dreamt of denying, it is by virtue of His essence or by virtue of a knowledge which was identical with His essence. As for material qualifications, hearing, sight and speech, they denied these completely, reckoning that the Koranic verses which gave God the qualification 'hearing' must be taken in a figurative sense; the same applied to verses attributing to God a 'hand', a term which had to be interpreted as signifying a 'benefit', in conformity with ancient Arabic usage. The Mu'tazilites thus revealed that they were very attached to certain passages of the Koran to which they gave a privileged position of a sort, so as to base their theodicy on them, but they had recourse to figurative interpretations to explain others, that is to say, those which did not fit in with their own system.

In the light of this theodicy, but also with a basis in some Koranic verses, they likewise denied the eternal, uncreated character of the Koran. It was 'the Word of God' but transmitted in Arabic, made up of sounds and phrases consisting of 'parts', that is, it was a word which, no more than the other attributes, could be considered as eternal and distinct at the risk of denying the fundamental divine unity. In the same way they refused to admit that God could be seen by the elect in paradise although many believers held this.

As well as insisting on divine unity, they also insisted on divine justice and on this ground defended human freewill. According to them, evil in whatever form could not be imputed to God; faults committed by man were entirely man's responsibility; as for the evil met with under different forms in the world, this could only be a semblance, and creation, the work of God, had no place for it. Man was thus fully free in his acts, and must suffer in full the consequences of the 'promise' made by God to the 'good' as well as the 'threat' made against the 'wicked'. Above all, this made it clear that no intercession was possible by the Prophet on behalf of believers who were sinners and that divine mercy could not have any more effect on them. The so-called principle of 'the promise and the threat', borrowed moreover from the Khārijites, resulted in making the believer face his responsibilities and in removing from him, as it were, all external means of appeal.

To this principle was bound that of the 'intermediate state' which eased the harshness of the purely Khārijite definition of 'believer'. If 'practice', that is, the observance of legal prescriptions, was considered essential and if simple verbal adherence to the doctrine of Islam was not sufficient, lapses in carrying out prescriptions did not always transform the 'believer' into an infidel and did not exclude him from the community, but placed him temporarily in a position apart.

To these reflections, which had for their starting-point the moral and religious life, were added still others of a philosophical nature. The principle of justice implied in fact that God would conform Himself to justice and would judge His creatures with equity, as regards good and evil. But it also implied that this good and evil could be known and defined by men themselves, thanks to their ability to reason. Thus the notions of justice and of moral good corresponded to the definitions given by human reason to which God is obliged to conform and His will found itself singularly limited by it. In one sense, Mu'tazilism ended up as a philosophical religion where reason was for a little raised to a position superior to that of the Divinity Himself. Certainly for its followers, there must not and there could not be conflict between God and the categories of human reason, but traditional religion was none the less considerably modified, since man was supposed to have access himself to the notion of good and evil, although in the current Muslim perspective this notion was determined by Revelation. This meant a diminution of prestige and usefulness for the Koranic message, at the same time as it was itself regarded as created.

The Mu'tazilites also had a further principle, that of 'commanding and prohibiting' according to which, the imām, leader of the community, had to prescribe firmly the recommended practices, and also sound belief, and to intervene likewise against bad practices and deviant ideas. If as a result they appeared close to Khārijism, they contented themselves to limit rebellion against the bad imām to certain circumstances, to wit, when his bad conduct was evident and when the undertaking had sufficient chances of succeeding.

The movement, whose thought with its radical opinions became gradually more coherent, met with remarkable success when the caliph, al-Ma'mūn, who had already begun to receive into his entourage some of its representatives, decided to impose as official doctrine its views, and in particular enjoined the cadis to adhere to the doctrine of the created Koran which constituted its most characteristic feature. At the same time the caliph undertook to reconcile the followers of Sunnism and Shi'ism. But the policy, to which he devoted himself with zeal and which he even wanted to impose by force, met with violent opposition which did not abate under his two like-minded successors, so much so, that al-Mutawakkil gave it up in 848. After this, the Mu'tazilites remained on the fringe except during the period of the Būyid emirs (945–1055) during which holders of very different politico-religious convictions confronted one another and briefly found an audience.

Thus their leading role came to an end, and it is easy to see, after this brief sketch of their history, how its significance can be interpreted in a variety of ways. Too often we have been content to see in it the manifestation of convictions, both philosophical and religious and close to rationalism, coming into conflict with the traditionalist current without supplanting it. Too often too, al-Ma'mūn has been cast in the role of enlightened ruler, open to the ideas of the ancient world and seeking to give Islam an appearance of conforming to the demands of reason: this explains why some orientalists have gone so far as to see the Mu'tazilites the 'freethinkers' (*Freidenker*) of Islam. From this it is but a short step to think of them as having carried the torch of rationalism against the obscurantism of traditional theologians, and this step was soon taken by admirers who made light of the reality of the available data.

If indeed it is beyond doubt that the Mu'tazilites were influenced by ancient philosophical thought, it also appears that they were at first much filled with the desire to defend Islam against rival doctrines. We know that one of them, al-Nazzām, was engaged in hot controversy with representatives of Manicheism which at this period was still alive in the Iranian and even Mesopotamian regions. Now the Manichean doctrine was strongly impregnated with neo-platonic gnosticism and it is understandable that, to refute it, the Mu'tazilites too had recourse to the armoury of Greek philosophy. We know, too, the controversies against Christianity in which they had engaged, and it is reported that the doctrine of the 'uncreated' Koran was, according to them, sufficient to bring about the accusation of associationism which they excluded by their definition of divine unity. Moreover the same definition safeguarded the creative freewill of God by stating that the world had not been created according to a 'pre-existing model', a criticism of positions of the Greek philosphers. Thus we can conclude that while they made use of the methods of the ancient thinkers and tried to give Islamic theological thought an aspect which was as satisfying to reason as possible, the Mu'tazilites remained faithfully attached to some simple principles formulated in the Koran, seeing in these the essence of their religion and so distancing themselves from any 'rationalist' conception as commonly understood.

On the other hand, these same Mu'tazilites were imbued with their 'philosophical system' and extended it by various considerations about the organisation of the world in which we find equally a very clear Greek influence. They proceeded to incite the caliph, al-Ma'mūn, to set up a veritable inquisition in order to impose their teaching. Sometimes we are amazed at the severity of the measures which were thus taken to get cadis, professional witnesses and principal doctors to adhere to their doctrines and more particularly to that of the 'created Koran'. Now this influence, hardly compatible with a real attempt at liberty of thought, can be explained very easily among militant Muslims. They were convinced of possessing the truth in a correct interpretation of Islam and remained in fact very close to the Khārijite revolutionaries who employed or advocated any means of furthering their cause. In spite of, or because of, their concern for logic and rigorism, the Mu'tazilites were as sectarian, in the modern sense of the term, as the followers of opposite tendencies. They were even more sectarian in so far as the success of their teaching seemed more important to them than maintaining the established order. This shows that it would be wrong to see in Mu'tazilism the ferment which, at a certain period, could have made Islam an 'enlightened' religion. It is true that Mu'tazilite tendencies were again found much later, in the twentieth century, among those who were then seeking to renew 'Islamic thought'; but those who took their inspiration from Mu'tazilism remained in any case very 'fundamentalist', which shows that Mu'tazilism should not be confused with any current of western thought but always be placed in the perspective in which it actually developed.

4 Other theological schools

Whatever might be in other respects the reactions with which the ardent proselytism of the Mu'tazilite caliphs clashed, it remains clear the the phenomenon itself profoundly influenced the evolution of medieval Islam. It was in relation to this teaching that other theological schools then took their stance and its fiercest adversaries themselves came to adopt its 'problematic' and to employ its methods of reasoning in order to expound their own systems. The Mu'tazilites had in fact been the first to deepen the theological problems, which until then had only flourished in particular circumstances, or which had not yet presented themselves clearly to the consciousness of believers, who were content to affirm, for example, that the Koran was 'the Word of God' without seeking to determine what such a formula implied. Perhaps it was necessary for their theories to come into being in order that other thinkers should come proposing and justifying contrary positions.

To the traditionalist reaction, which showed itself under the caliphate of al-Ma'mūn and which was inspired by Aḥmad Ibn Hanbal in particular, consisted in taking mainly the opposite stance to Mu'tazilite affirmations. This anti-rationalist theology was expressed in creeds, often very short, which merely enumerated the principal articles necessary, and by their conciseness, were in contrast to the developments attributed to the Mu'tazilite thinkers. The elements invoked were drawn from the collections of the traditions such as those of Ibn Hanbal, who was considered, by his adversaries, as a simple traditionist and as having no right, according to them, to the rank of jurisconsult still less to that of 'theologian'. In fact, Ibn Hanbal impugned the authenticity of this discipline which was really still in embryo, and the creeds of the 'traditionalist' tendency – this is the general term most convenient for designating them because some came from persons who were not disciples of Ibn Hanbal – vigorously affirmed the harmful character of controversy and reasoning in matters of faith; to discuss with an adversary, Ibn Hanbal would have declared, is always to risk ending up in compromise and to be led to make concessions, which is not acceptable.

Discussion in itself, for the holders of this view, has moreover no justification. It is necessary to believe, they repeated, 'what God has said', notably 'what God has said of Himself', then to hold on to the obvious sense of the texts; this is a literalist, but also a fundamentalist, position, for it is to the Koran, to the traditions and to the usages admitted by the Companions that one refers exclusively from now on, while giving the least possible scope to personal interpretation. One must believe in God and believe that He is such as He described Himself, accepting the terms which God applies to Himself in the Koranic text, and also the expressions He uses when speaking of Himself, such as 'His face', 'His hand' and 'His throne', and one must do this without trying to understand how such expressions can be appropriate to Him when they are also applied to creatures. One must also believe that the Koran is uncreated, in as much as it is the 'Word of God'. One must affirm that God is the creator of everything, and that in consequence the 'divine decree' has to do with evil as well as good, and that God is the creator of human actions, whether they are good or bad. One must finally declare that faith 'increases or decreases' according to acts performed, and this implies that the believer, from the moment he accepts the Islamic faith, cannot be excluded from the community for any failure whatsoever.

The old Murji'ite tendency was thus revived in such creeds, since they aimed at maintaining at all costs the unity of the community and avoiding mutual condemnations and splits. A conception of authority was also arrived at which impugned every movement of rebellion; it was necessary to obey the imām in all circumstances and to be willing to pray behind him, whatever the occasion and whether the imām was pious or impious, as long as he was a believer.

A similar literalist and fideist belief which opposed any research into the 'why' of things fits in, in fact, with one of the constants of ordinary Islamic thought. It continued to inspire the Hanbalite school and appeared, for example, among the Mālikites of the West. However it did not escape the influence, in the course of time, of Mu'tazilism and the rationalist theology which grew up in its wake. One then saw the growth of veritable 'theological treatises' which presented their objects of faith in a more elaborate form and which made room, as an introduction, for a kind of theory of knowledge. Philosophical reflexion only showed itself timidly in these traditionalist works, and that was despite the initial refusal of discussion which we have already mentioned. But the traditionalists none the less maintained their fundamental positions, notably the existence of divine 'attributes', distinct and eternal, expressed by nouns in close relation to the adjectives used in the Koranic text. Thus they affirmed vigorously that God possessed Life, Power, Knowledge, Speech, since the Koran affirmed that God was living, powerful, knowing, speaking. What is more, they engaged in battle with the followers of Shi'ism and, in order to balance the veneration of the imāms which one found in these circles, they set out to commend a real devotion to the persons of the Companions in so far as they were the guardians of ancient custom. The 'community' had taken for them a primary importance, since the community, extending the action of the Prophet, was the real guarantor of the sound interpretation of Islam and of the perfect application of its rules. From this there resulted, as a political attitude, adherence to the principle of the designation of the imām by the community or by its principal representatives. There also resulted from it a particular legal methodology since the traditionalists considered as 'source' of the Law, after the Koran and the Prophet's custom, the 'consensus' of the Companions and of the 'early Muslims'. From this came the name of 'people of the *sunna* and the community' which they generally bore and in which the term 'community' was the most important.

This traditionalist tendency, which was above all represented by the Hanbalite school, but which also found other forms of expression, maintained itself all through the history. Firmly rooted in Baghdad and in Iraq, it appeared equally in Syria and elsewhere. The conflict, which never ceased to oppose it to Mu'tazilism, resulted however in producing yet another tendency, that which corresponded to the growth of the speculative theology which was progressively used, from the beginning of the tenth century, to deal with doctrinal questions. The school which grew out of this took the name of Ash'arite from the name of al-Ash'ari, to whom is attributed its founding, even though al-Ash'ari may only have been a Mu'tazilite who, as a result of circumstances unknown to us, abjured solemnly his first convictions to follow the traditionalist theses. Undertaking to defend himself against the adversaries of all kinds whom he might meet, not only his old friends the Mu'tazilites but also the Zoroastrians, the Manicheans, even the Christians, he challenged the principle stated by the Hanbalites, according to which one must avoid all polemic, and it is reported that for this reason his adherence to traditionalism was not considered authentic. For all that, his attitude accounts for the fact that he effectively undertook, in theological treatises which can be regarded as the oldest of the genre – apart from the Mu'tazilite treatises not preserved – to substantiate the different articles of faith by listing in each case the proofs available: the Koran, the tradition, and also reasoning. Thus the existence of God, according to al-Ash'ari, could be proved by reason, which only confirms the teaching of revelation. Doubtless this theology was still very rudimentary but the very fact that he had recourse to it underlines the originality of the position of al-Ash'ari in comparison with that of Ibn Hanbal and his disciples who, even when they put forward a creed, avoided giving rational arguments.

Thus the question has often been discussed as to whether al-Ash'ari was or was not the true founder of the dogmatic theology known as *kalām*, taken from an Arabic word meaning 'speech' and 'discussion'. In fact, we are dealing with a false problem for, if it is clear that the first treatises of dogmatic theology only appeared with al-Ash'ari's disciples, it is no less certain that the personal attitude of al-Ash'ari alone allowed this later development. It is also more important to note how the Ash'arites, who at first adhered fully to traditionalist theses, except when it dealt with the prohibition of discussion, gradually came to be more flexible in their formulations, sometimes adopting, at the doctrinal level, theses forming a 'just mean'; an example is the case of freewill, as regards which, following their master, they succeeded in elaborating a doctrine which took into account some of their adversaries' objections. While accepting the analysis of the Mu'tazilites who distinguished the ability to act from the act itself, they declared in effect that the ability could not exist before the act but that ability and act must be simultaneous. In this way the human act was at the same time considered to be a free act because 'acquired' by the man who appropriates it, and is responsible for it, and to be an act willed by God. In this way the traditional thesis is preserved and divine omnipotence affirmed while at the same time, freewill and the problematic of the Mu'tazilites is accepted but used against them. In the same way, the

Ash'arites defended the reality of the divine 'attributes', while accepting at the same time the distinction introduced by some Mu'tazilites between the attributes of the essence and the attributes of action, which implied regarding the latter as 'temporal' since they were occasional. Further, while accepting the uncreated character of the Koran as text, they considered that the Koran, as written or pronounced by human beings, was 'created'. And some of them, such as the famous al-Ghazāli, went so far as to apply to the Koran the distinction made in respect of man between the interior word or unexpressed idea, and the external word. As to the attributes of essence, they affirmed their eternal reality while declaring that these attributes were different from those which could be applied to man.

Thus putting aside the objections raised by the advocates of 'reason', the Ash'arites sometimes noticeably modified traditional positions. They remained none the less faithful supporters of 'Abbāsid legitimism, although their attitude might often appear suspect to the actual rulers. Thus between the tenth and thirteenth centuries they constituted the principal school of what may be called the Sunnite *kalām*, recognising the rights and the outstanding worth of the first caliphs, and likewise preaching loyalty as regards later caliphs. They were, however, not alone in defending such ideas, and alongside Ash'arism, another parallel school of Sunnite theology came into being, whose origin is attributed to a contemporary of al-Ash'ari called al-Māturīdi and who lived in Transoxiana. This Māturīdism, tied to the Hanafite legal school, only came to real fruition at a much later period and in somewhat marginal regions, but its interpretation of fundamental dogmas was close to that defended by the Ash'arites and on this ground is worthy of mention.

5 Shi'ism

The theological controversies we have just been discussing had remained strangely dependent, in spite of their abstract character, on political questions, such as the problem presented to the first community by the emergence of this Shi'ism, whose followers, as we have already seen, had wanted to defend the claims of 'Ali to the caliphate. Shi'ism, for its part, also presented varied aspects and soon split up into various branches with different political and doctrinal options. These branches, in order that their ideas might prevail, preserved one common habit, that of preferring to resort to rational arguments and to employ them alongside the traditions legitimising for them, from the beginning, the rights of 'Ali, the successor whom in their view the Prophet, in his lifetime, had himself designated for this office. Thus it was in respect of the right to the imāmate and of its legal transmission that in the course of time differences and debates appeared.

One group of Shi'ites, who were called Zaydites after the oldest claimant whose cause they supported, was distinguished, for example, by maintaining that the imām should manifest himself among the members of 'Ali's posterity by the extent that he showed exceptional qualities of piety, knowledge and courage; this excluded every form of designation and of hereditary principle, but preserved the possibility of legitimism. The representatives of two other trends who took the name of Imāmite and Isma'ilite, believed on the contrary in the existence of a line of imāms descended from 'Ali and Fātima who were designated from father to son until the last, the twelfth for the former, the seventh for the latter, had disappeared. Thus the former awaited the 'return' of an imām, the twelfth, who disappeared in 873, and whose return is to be accompanied by the establishment of a just order and by punishment of all those who were opposed to his followers. The latter thought that from the seventh imām, the son of a certain Ismā'īl who had disappeared in the previous century, there descended a line of 'hidden' imāms, one of whom would, one fine day, also appear to establish justice.

While the Imāmites, also called 'Twelvers', are awaiting, even today, the reappearance of their last imām as 'Mahdi', the Ismā'īlis, for their part, saw an imām or pretended imām, claim this title and in 909 found the Fātimid caliphate of Ifriqiya which later moved to Egypt (969–1171). At first, then, both developed messianic hopes in the same way, but these hopes were attenuated or transformed among the Ismā'īlis, while they became more marked among the Imāmites who regarded all political and religious life as depending on them. The imām expected by these latter must, like his predecessors, be endowed with superhuman qualities, infallible and sinless, an undisputed guide in the full sense of the word, guardian of a truth not necessarily the same as that corresponding to the obvious sense of the official Koranic message. Imāmite Shi'ism, then, could have been led to adopt the theory of a divine voluntarism and it may even have been tempted to try this road. In fact, in circumstances not yet very clear, it allied itself with the rationalist tendency in Mu'tazilism, attacking the anthropomorphic interpretations and considering the truth, of which the imām is guardian, as a truth fully in accordance with reason.

Analogous attitudes of opposition, or at least of reserve, with regard to the official version of the revealed text, seem to have been at the roots of this rapprochement between Shi'ism and a Mu'tazilism which did not hesitate moreover to criticise the established Sunnite order. Imāmism was both rationalising and intellectualist, and hoped for the parousia without intervening effectively at the level of action. Very inward-looking, it was tempted to cultivate moroseness and tragedy. The imāms were all considered to be the innocent victims of the Sunni caliphs, having all died violently or by poison. The tragedy of the death of al-Husayn at Kerbela gave rise to theatrical representations recalling the passion plays of the medieval West. The Imāmites thus delighted in meditating on the past misfortunes of the chosen Family, while their thinkers insisted on the esoteric doctrine which supported the whole of the system and recommended a spiritual life founded on the knowledge of the secrets and on the imitation of the imāms. Starting from earlier traditions, mentioned especially by the authors of the tenth century, a theosophy was formed which occupied a more important place in the thought of the movement as Imāmism moved away from political action.

Ismā'īlism, on the other hand, experienced in this latter respect brilliant successes since it produced the Fātimid caliphate which was to rule, at first in Ifriqiya then in Egypt, for more than three centuries. It was none the less tied to a very elaborate philosophical defence of its positions which at one and the same time justified the superhuman nature of the imāms or caliphs and the cycle of their disappearance and reappearance. Its esoteric teaching, reserved for the initiated, adapted the emanationist system of the philosophers of late antiquity to Koranic truths, making the imām an emanation of the universal Spirit which governs the world. In teaching directed towards propaganda, the accent was placed more on philosophical speculations than on the demands of the spiritual life, a tendency which only increased with the neo-Ismā'īlism preached in the eleventh century at Alamut in Iran: the imām here became in effect superior to the Prophet and to the Law, since it fell to the imām to promulgate a new revelation which would inaugurate a new era. The superiority of Muhammad, respected by Imāmism, was thus deliberately set aside by the extremist branches of Ismā'īlism.

6 The mystical current

Other religous or intellectual currents had equally come into being, which were less dependent on the political choices of their followers but which, too, formed essential elements in Islamic thought. First of all there was the ascetic and mystical movement commonly called Sūfism, from the word 'sufi' which appears to have been given to the woollen cloak worn by the first ascetics. Sūfism presented itself, alongside legal and theological disciplines, as a particular 'way' aiming at a state of perfection and sanctity which the believer was able to achieve by renouncing the world and by seeking ecstasy. This way had its roots deep in certain practices of the early Islamic period and was based on Koranic teachings. In addition to those verses which regulated in precise fashion liturgical life and social relations, other passages of the revealed text vehemently condemned the acquisition of riches, and kept a privileged place in Paradise for certain elect. Encouraged by the possibility, also mentioned in the Koran, that the believer might come closer to his Lord, the ambition of the Sūfis soon became to be numbered among those 'brought near' (*muqarrabūn*) who had been particularly distinguished by God. But in the course of the centuries Sūfism sometimes took forms very different from one another, and in these some have seen the effect of diversity of heritage; sometimes, too, they were regarded as suspect by scholars and governors.

It is certain, for example, that the current represented by individuals such as al-Hasan al-Basri (d. 722) or al-Muhāsibi (d. 857) whose name (or surname) recalls the 'self-examination' (*muhāsaba*) which he had recommended, did not fail to show some analogies with the asceticism which had been practised in the East by the Christian Cenobites. For her part, the famous Rābi'a (d. 801) sang of the divine love in accents which could recall those of other mystics of the eastern church; and the Egyptian Dhū-l-Nūn (d. 859), of Coptic origin, traced an itinerary of the stages of the journey of the soul invaded by joy, which has been compared with that of a Christian author.

Other Sūfis, such as the Iranian al-Bistāmi (d. 874) or Junayd (d. 910), were led to describe the mystical union as a state of annihilation of the I (*fanā*) or rather of the 'inherence' (*hulūl*) of God in the human soul; another, the celebrated al-Hallāj who was condemned to death for heresy in 922, was able to exclaim, for example: 'I am the Truth' (*anā l-haqq*). In such outbursts, some Islamic scholars were led to see the influence either of Indian doctrines or of the gnosticism which had persisted particularly in Iran through the intermediacy of Manicheism. Still later, while brotherhoods appeared which brought together men from different backgrounds and emphasised exercises such as litanies (under the form of repetitions of the name of God called *dhikr*) and concerts of spiritual music, Sūfism took on two quite distinct aspects, that of the theologians and that of the theosophists. The former, such as the great al-Ghazāli (d. 1111) joined to their quest for knowledge a concern for a spiritual life directed towards the love of God; the latter, like al-Suhrawardi (d. 1191) looked for the 'realising illumination' at the centre of a theosophy to which we shall return, or again, like Ibn 'Arabi (d. 1240) did not hesitate to affirm their attachment to an existential monism.

Sūfism as such has therefore most certainly incorporated ideas borrowed from foreign teaching. But since Louis Massignon in particular was given to emphasise the 'Koranic germs' of the movement, hardly anyone has contested the originality of this school of spirituality peculiar to Islam, whose study however demands much discernment: its adherents professed in fact doctrines often difficult to interpret and which are only distinguished from one another by delicate nuances. Typical is the case of al-Hallāj; he was executed after a remarkable trial in which doctrinal accusations and political suspicions were mingled, and has continued to be divisive for the Muslim conscience, having both followers and detractors in the very heart of what is considered the Sunnite community attached to traditionalism. In spite of or because of his celebrated formula 'I am the Truth', he was regarded by some as faithful to orthodoxy and accused by others of 'Manicheism', as it was called at that period. And the orientalists have continued to be divided about his remarks, even after the warm plea on his behalf written by Louis Massignon.

The position of this same al-Hallāj regarding Christianity remains, on the other hand, difficult to define, despite the famous statement which has been explained by Louis Massignon under the form 'It is under the supreme authority of the Cross that I die' but which should be more correctly translated 'It is in the religion of the gibbet that I die', since the word designating 'cross' also applies to the 'gibbet' on which those condemned to death in Islamic countries were tortured. That al-Hallāj may have in some way sought martyrdom and sacrificed himself to the divine Love which he preached, while trying to remain faithful to traditional teaching, cannot be doubted; but nothing allows us to affirm that he was deliberately referring to the religion of Christ;

The two preceding translations of the same phrase illustrate admirably the nature of the difficulties one is up against when trying to understand and place correctly the statements of mystics fond of hyperbole. Nothing also shows more clearly the latent opposition which always existed in Islam between the ecstatic Sūfis and the rigid legal thinkers. However, we must not minimise the influence that such individuals were able to exert on the mass of believers. If they survive today chiefly by written works which are sometimes spiritual classics, they formerly had disciples who ensured the direct transmission of their thought. Thus the different streams of Sūfism spread by initiation, but at the same time certain sermons of this kind managed to touch the masses immediately and more widely. One, Sulami (d. 1021), left, for example, two kinds of work, one meant for novices, the other advocating an ethic which could be practised by all. Even al-Hallāj had thought it a good idea to preach in the markets, witnessing to his personal experience, but also calling on his contemporaries to reform themselves morally, and not scorning to further his ideas also among the rulers. Later the separation made itself more clearly felt between those who looked to a gnostic theosophy reserved for a few, and those who strove to make the ascetic and mystic 'way' accessible to the masses. If, for example, al-Ghazāli recognised that some were destined to live in the world, he none the less thought it important to propagate among them the Sūfi ideal, which for his part he integrated into the traditional teaching, and to define for their benefit a Sūfi ethic which he hoped to see widely adopted.

The relations between men of religion and mystics, marked from the beginning by reserve and ambiguity, thus did not cease to grow stronger in the course of time, and despite verbal utterances, condemning some of its representatives. Sūfism spread more and more from about the twelfth century, chiefly thanks to the brotherhoods. Certain doctors, filled with intellectualist ideas, like the Mu'tazilite or Promu'tazilite Hanafites, certainly continued to keep themselves aloof. But the Shāfi'ites, on the other hand, were for the most part seduced, and it is not by chance that they often acted as its champions at the heart of the Muslim community. The Hanbalites, moreover, less eager to interiorise the actions of the cult and more critical of the exhibitionism of some mystics, none the less showed themselves to be willingly in agreement with the moral rules pronounced by the Sūfis and also with their ideal of renunciation. One of the most famous founders of an order in the twelfth century, 'Abd al-Qādir al-Jīlāni, was a well-known Hanbalite and many Hanbalites joined the various confraternities which were created in the thirteenth and fourteenth centuries. At this period the mystical movement inspired theological choices and very lively forms of piety at the heart of the Islamic community, guaranteeing a role which was to grow even more in the centuries to come.

7 The philosophical current

Eventually the philosophical current appeared clearly distinct, and it too had its influence on the more traditional religious customs after having merged, as we have seen, with the divisions in political life. It was chiefly at the beginning of the ninth century that the philosophical treatises of the Greek authors of the classical period or of late antiquity began to be translated into Arabic and known in cultured circles, sometimes with a false attribution, since the famous *Theology* attributed to Aristotle was in fact a neoplatonic treatise. The Mu'tazilites, who then had the ear of the caliph al-Ma'mūn, seem to have been the chief instigators of this activity of translation which had certainly begun earlier, thanks to Syriac-Christian circles, but which was greatly increased with the creation of the academy called the House of Wisdom. The Muslim thinkers, who were inspired by the works thus translated to elaborate their doctrine, were given the name of *faylasūf* (from the Greek *philosophos*) and the discipline called *falsafa* designates more particularly the philosophy of Greek inspiration, as opposed to the theosophy preferred by the mystics.

The positions defended by these philosophers, like those held by some Sūfis, could not but create moral dilemmas for the Muslim community, and they themselves experienced some difficulties in reconciling with dogma the doctrines they had taken over from the Greeks. That is to say that they lived without exception on the periphery of the world of the men of religion, who did not accept them as being of themselves. While recognising what was given in revelation and reckoning that revelation and reason could not but agree, they gave a place to reason that many of the believers, even if they were Mu'tazilites, could not generally admit, since they based their cosmology and their ethic entirely on reason.

It is true that the idea of a necessary agreement between reason and revelation was in itself widely spread among Muslim thinkers. But the majority among them were to adopt it in the ethical realm where the Koranic prescriptions agreed quite well with the moral counsels taken from earlier civilisations; in the realm of faith they stuck to revelation, and only some among them experienced the need, as we have seen, to support themselves by rational arguments in order to defend the articles of this faith and to treat reason, when they had recourse to it, as a 'handmaid of theology'. Different, then, was the opinion of the philosophers, each of whom conceived his own system independently of all revealed truth, aided only by the deep conviction of a pre-existing harmony, and who met a different fate for having known more or less well how to assuage the reticences of their contemporaries.

The first of these *faylasūf* was undoubtedly al-Kindi (d. about 873), who lived in Baghdad at the time of the Mu'tazilite caliphs and who was linked with the representatives of this tendency, without, however, belonging to their group. If it still remains difficult to get an overall idea of his teaching through the numerous opuscula in which he expressed it, we know that he wished to preserve a special place for prophetic knowledge distinct from purely human science and held that there were two forms of knowledge which ought to be in harmony. He adopted the neoplatonic theory which declared that the world emanated from God through the intermediacy of a hierarchy of several intelligences, while maintaining the principle of creation *ex nihilo*, which alone was compatible with Koranic teaching, and only bringing in emanation at a second stage. Similarly he explained in one of his treatises the Greek theory of the four intellects but tried to safeguard the idea of divine transcendence.

More daring and more fully formulated, on the other hand, appeared the thought of al-Fārābi, who stayed in Aleppo at the court of the Hamdanid emirs and died in Damascus in 950, after having been the author of extensive treatises which have been partially preserved for us. His doctrine was derived at one and the same time from Plato and from a neoplatonism attributed by tradition to Aristotle; it was in effect from the wisdom of the ancient Greeks, wrongly considered to be a homogenous whole, that he had drawn inspiration, without however ceasing to profess a Muslim faith which he identified with the highest expression of human reason.

Thus he defended a metaphysic of essence, which considered existence as an accident, and which distinguished between necessary Being and possible beings which come into existence thanks to the Necessary Being. It was accompanied by a theory of Intelligences which emanated the one from the other, the first ones emanating from the Necessary Being, the last irradiating forms into matter and being at the origin of the world. In this system, the human intellect, which also proceeds from this tenth intelligence, passes through three stages, possible, actual, and acquired; but the conception of al-Fārābi remained coloured by neoplatonism in the sense that the acquired intellect was able to enter into contact with the 'active' intelligence without using the senses. Finally the management of the 'Ideal City', to which al-Fārābi dedicated a famous treatise, must, according to him, be entrusted to an imām who, as successor of a prophet, would establish laws and appear under the guise of a wise man, imām-philosopher and prophet, uniting each to the active Intelligence in ways which remained different.

The philosophy of al-Fārābi, thus justifying Revelation without however placing itself about it, constituted the first coherent attempt at harmonising Islamic religion and human wisdom. But it is not pointless to note the analogies which existed between the ideas which it used and those of the Shi'ites. These analogies are not surprising when one imagines that such a philosophy came into being at the court of the Hamdanids who themselves professed the Imāmite doctrine; al-Fārābi's theories, while placing themselves on an intellectual plane, suffered the effects of the politico-religious preoccupations favoured in the environment where they were developed.

After al-Fārābi, *falsafa* was cultivated by numerous men of letters who insisted on this or that conceptual aspect without adding any important innovation. Such was in a sense the role of Miskawayh (d. 1030) who interested himself more particularly in moral, theoretical and practical problems, while remaining faithful to the mystical flights which had already animated al-Fārābi and which gave his ethical prescriptions their meaning. But the most striking philosopher was without doubt the famous Ibn Sīnā, known in the West under the name of Avicenna (d. 1037), a great physician as well as a great thinker, who also fulfilled political functions in the service of various princes of Iran.

Avicenna took up again the distinction drawn by al-Fārābi between essence and existence and drew some fresh logical conclusions; he was thus led to change the idea of 'creation' slightly. This could only be for him the result of a necessary activity of the Being who thinks Himself, the knowledge which the divinity has of itself constituting the first emanation, the first Intelligence, from which the other intelligences are derived and eventually the world. As to human intelligences, they proceed from the tenth intelligence which alone permits the intellect to abstract the intelligible from the sensible and to raise itself eventually to the degree of sainthood or prophethood. Avicenna, just like al-Fārābi, was a mystic and believed that the soul's destiny was to unite itself to the superior being from which it received illumination – whence the name illuminative philosophy which he himself gave to his doctrine – without, however, the fate of the soul in the beyond being determined.

There is nothing surprising, then, in that the theologians concerned with orthodoxy set out to fight against this *falsafa* which had the greatest difficulty in respecting the fundamental articles of the dogma: creation *ex nihilo*, the resurrection of bodies, and the personal survival of the soul. The great al-Ghazāli particularly distinguished himself in this criticism of the philosophers, from whom moreover he sometimes took over the methods of argumentation.

Falsafa nevertheless found a talented protagonist in the Islamic West, in the person of Ibn Rushd or Averroes (d. 1198) who was a judge in Spain and a counsellor of the Almohad rulers, but this did not prevent him at the end of his life from being the butt of attack by men of religion. Averroes is difficult to interpret because his work, known above all through translations made by Spanish rabbis, owes its prestige today to the influence which it exerted in medieval Europe where it was presented as the expression of a doctrine of double truth. In fact, Ibn Rushd, like many Muslim thinkers, thought that there existed several levels of understanding a revealed text such as the Koran, and that it was not good to spread abroad profound ideas among ignorant people. Thus he practised an esotericism which made of the philosophical truth reserved for the initiates, the true sense of a revealed message of which the common people could comprehend only the apparent significance. This method permitted him to reconcile faith and philosophy, this last being conceived by him as a return to the Aristotelianism to which his predecessors had not always been faithful.

The esotericism of Ibn Rushd was in any case quite different from that of al-Suhrawardi who, at the same period in the East (he died in 1191 at Aleppo, victim of Saladin's hostility) elaborated an 'illuminative or oriental wisdom' which he treated as a prolongation of Avicennian doctrine, although it drew its inspiration from ancient Persia and was in opposition to the peripatetic philosophy of the westerners. It was a spiritual way which al-Suhrawardi offered to those not satisfied by either the discourses of the 'peripatetics' nor those of the dialectical theologians, a spiritual way leading to the revelation of intelligible lights by the annihilation of the cognitive *I*. This theosophy took on a special importance in Islam because it was at the source of a whole philosophico-mystical current which developed particularly among the Iranian thinkers and which reached its full development from the sixteenth century onwards.

8 Schisms in history

Such currents of thought, each dependent on the prevalence of disciplines such as law, the science of traditions, theology, mysticism and philosophy, which, theoretically, were not rivals but complementary, increased in fact, according to the favourable climate existing here and there, through the differences rampant in the heart of each branch and dividing their chief representatives. Competition asserted itself much more keenly, as each scholar or thinker was led to regard the sciences which he did not practise as inferior, and the currents of thought to which he did not adhere as erroneous. It is in this sense that there was propagated rapidly in Muslim circles the idea of a truth which could only be fully attained by a definite method, that of one of the disciplines or doctrines in question. We see this fact in particular appearing in the famous 'autobiography' of al-Ghazāli which, if it did not perhaps describe real events, none the less constitutes a 'spiritual journey' characteristic of the preoccupations of the scholars of this period. Al-Ghazāli, after having successively withdrawn from the paths proposed by the Ismā'īli doctrine and the philosophy, which he condemned outright, and also by the law and the theology, in which he recognised only a relative value, discovered in Sūfism the only road by which to attain saving truth.

In the development of these currents of thought, it was not just a matter of reflections or discussions relative to the best way of knowledge, and leading to the composition of polemical writings or the pursuit of intellectual and academic jousting. Such conflicts were in fact bound up, as we have seen, with the schisms which took place in the heart of Islam and which often took on dramatic dimensions in so far as their character was political as well as religious, the liveliest of these schisms corresponding to the Sunnite-Shi'ite conflict. Indeed Shi'ism, while possessing a doctrine which in the course of time became more precise and more diversified, wanted at first to gain power for the imāms. If the Imāmites did not succeed in this, they fermented serious trouble at certain periods – in particular the period of the Būyid emirs in Baghdad; the Zaydites were able to establish principalities in Daylam and in the Yemen; above all, the Ismā'īlis founded the Fātimid caliphate; all political changes expressed themselves in these various states by internal struggles whose manifestations reflected the sectarianism of the time.

Since the external sign of belonging to Shi'ism or Sunnism consisted in the formula adopted in the call to prayer, the muezzins were more than once victims of ill-usage for having chosen the formula which did not please, or no longer pleased, the rulers or the masses. Similarly, at Baghdad in the tenth century, the Shi'ites wanted to profit from the goodwill of the Būyid emirs to celebrate publicly their two greatest feasts, that of 10 Muharram commemorating the death of al-Husayn at Kerbela and that of Dhū-l-Hijja which commemorated the episode of Ghadīr Khumm in the course of which Muhammad was said to have designated 'Ali as his successor; but they came up against the opposition of the Sunnites who did everything they could to stop the holding of such ceremonies. The popular confrontations were so brutal that the authorities had to resign themselves to forbidding these celebrations. Later in Syria, when the dynasties arising from the Seljuk domination imposed their authority and re-established Sunnism in a country which had passed under the Shi'ite rod, bitter reprisals were not slow in appearing. One example of this was what happened when the prince of Aleppo built a madrasa or college of higher education destined to produce Sunni professors and when the Shi'ites hastened to demolish the building as it was being constructed. The new governors none the less pursued their policy, and Damascus especially witnessed the massacre of

Ismā'īlis who continued to resist. These same Ismā'īlis practised in Iran, where they had no more success in triumphing over their enemies, a kind of terrorism which, it would seem, struck at great personages such as certain viziers of the first Seljuk sultans. The quarrels between Sunnis and Shi'ites were thus at the root of numerous troubles and armed assaults which cannot be understood apart from a latent division of spirits, on which local struggles and ambitions did not cease to feed.

In addition there were the schisms and tensions existing at the centre of the two great Sunnite and Shi'ite blocs, which were stirred up by diverse intellectual tendencies but which were none the less monolithic in action. The leaders dispensed their favours according to their personal choices. In Sunnite circles, for example, the followers of the two Ash'arite and Hanbalite schools, who often confronted each other in Baghdad in the Seljuk period, were supported, the one by the sultans, the other by the caliphs. Moreover, the recommendations of the caliph in doctrinal matters did not have the value of orders, especially at a time when the real power was in large part monopolised by the sultans. Certainly the opinion of the caliph had previously carried more weight in this sphere, and we have seen that al-Ma'mūn did not hesitate to maintain a religious policy contrary to the then prevalent opinion. But he himself had failed to convince the majority of men of religion to conform to it, and the situation was always ambiguous regarding what one is tempted to call the doctrinal magisterium in Sunnite Islam. Hence the continual troubles which marked 'Abbāsid society even when there was no question of revolutionary intrigues or downright revolts but simply of conflicts between holders of different theological positions.

The same climate of opposition prone to insurrection, and of instability, prevailed in the provinces won over to Shi'ism. There also there were confrontations between multiple movements which did not understand each other and even attacked each other through propaganda without adopting an analogous policy in respect of the Sunnite Baghdadian power. The Fātimids of Egypt and the Carmathians of

Bahrein, for example, although stemming from the same Ismā'īli branch, did not combine at the moment when they sent expeditions against the caliphate which could have been made jointly. All the more reason for there never having been the least unity of action between adherents of the same Shi'ite ideology who differed from one another on an essential point, the name and person of the imām on whom fell the direction of the community. Their manoeuvres followed or paralleled one another in the complex mosaic of movements opposing the 'Abbāsid caliphate.

For their part again, the followers of spiritual or intellectual currents such as Sufism or *falsafa* did not hesitate to affirm their political preferences and very often had difficulties with the established authorities, especially the Sunnites. We know of several cases of Sūfis condemned to death for heterodoxy, al-Hallāj in 922, al-Hamadhāni in 1131, al-Suhrawardi in 1191. And if the philosophers were less ill-treated, this was because their teaching hardly touched the masses and they rarely had the opportunity of spreading their ideas in public places. Thus they could be protected by princes who were often Shi'ites, and who called themselves 'enlightened', without this appearing to cause disquiet to public opinion.

The reciprocal situation of these various currents and movements of all kinds thus experienced different stages, determined in part by the interplay of the factions to which they had given rise. But there remains the fact that the exact part played by the properly doctrinal choices in the attitudes and designs of the rulers of the period can only be known with difficulty. Schisms and political interests merged, often inextricably, with the effects of social tensions, to bring about events which the violence of opposing ideas made to follow one another in accelerating rhythm. The same ideas were reflected in the works of the literati (*adīb*), who left a profound mark on the civilisation of which they were the least favoured form of expression.

Thus Jāhiz was preoccupied, not only with enhancing the Arab heritage and stigmatising the oddities of the Persians, but also with defending the Mu'tazilite doctrine of which he was a fervent follower and to which he refers more or less explicitly throughout his great encyclopedic work on animals. The anthologist Ibn Qutayba was also interested as much in problems of theological order as in the various stories he collected. A century later, at the time of the Būyid emirs, a period of relative tolerance when philosophy appears to have attracted many men of letters, we find al-Tawhīdi, a talented stylist and narrator, in dialogue with the philosopher Miskawayh whose ethic he appreciated while showing at the same time a marked liking for Sūfism; if al-Tawhīdi was seduced by Greek logic, he defended himself against it in order to preserve the fathomless mystery of the divinity. For the rest, the philosophers themselves such as Miskawayh or Ibn Sīnā, while constructing apparently rationalistic systems, remained attracted by the mystical flights which, in their case, took on a philosophical look. Nearly all the writers were thus preoccupied with religious or politico-religious problems, witness those authors of comic playlets such as al-Hamadāni, whose heroes very often take it out on the followers of some religious sect. Even the poets, when not composing bacchic or erotic poetry, made themselves the panegyrists of the defenders of Islam or of the holders of the caliphate by indulging in a veritable politico-religious propaganda, sometimes of Shi'ite tendency, or again sang the merits of asceticism. In Arabic literature we find an echo of the heterogeneous nature of the Islamic world and of the struggles of warring influences which made themselves felt between groups of different ethnic origin; it also mirrored faithfully the controversies which did not cease to accompany the development of medieval Islamic thought.

Thus we can understand, in the face of such a disturbed doctrinal history, that the orientalists may have been tempted to give some degree of priority to their own subjects of interest, defending the authors whose distinctive positions they had penetrated, emphasising the data furnished by a single category of sources and adding yet again to the complexity of a multiple picture. It will suffice to recall how certain among them spoke highly, as we have seen, of Mu'tazilism where they tried to see a 'rational' interpretation of Islam; others only paid attention to Ash'arism, a form of orthodox theology whose role they compared to that played by Thomism in the Christian West. Others again came to be particularly interested either in the traditionalist theology of the Hanbalite sort, whose place had at first for long been played down, or in the later theosophy which appeared to them to be the culmination of a religion based on prophecy. Still others loved to insist on the legal nature of an Islam where the liturgical acts and social relations were assessed by means of a precise code leaving adequate room for the intention of the faithful; while some did not cease to praise the eminent virtue of a Sūfism which allowed them to point out resemblances between Muslim and Christian mysticism. Few among them in any case knew how to deal with the multiplicity of the doctrinal aspects of medieval Islam and to preserve a sufficiently comprehensive vision of the whole.

Only such a vision allows us to understand the evolution of the great currents of thought. Each one of them, indeed, while obeying its own logic, formulated its doctrine with reference to the movements which it fought. To take a significant example: it was because he attacked *falsafa* that al-Ghazāli adopted philosophical languages and modes of reasoning, thus committing the Ash'arite theology to a new road; and perhaps his fight against Ismā'īlism may also explain in certain measure his taste for an interiorisation restricted to the initiated. It was because he fought fiercely against Mu'tazilism that a traditionalist like Abū Ya'lā, in the eleventh century, adopted a problematic that can be described as rationalising. It is important then to take note of this complex and changing situation and to place each reaction in the context of the politico-religious polemics of the time, in order to place correctly the tendencies which the primary object of this chapter has been to define.

CHAPTER 4

Islam and the political order

We have seen how often the doctrine of Islam experienced, in the course of the Middle Ages, successive and rival expressions, as controversies and opposing views caused it to define itself gradually in sometimes differing directions. We have also seen the role played in this respect by the political problems which were the source of the first rifts to appear among the Muslims, and which gave a direction to some of their thinking. It is thus understandable that the types of government which had been created in the various Islamic countries in the Middle Ages, and whose appearance often depended on doctrinal choices previously made, deserve, in their turn, to be considered in a historic perspective.

This perspective will insist first of all on the variety of regimes which followed each other at the heart of the empire from the Prophet's death to the Mongol invasion and until the present day. Not only was it the rule of the first 'rightly guided' caliphs which soon gave place to the forms of government maintained first by the Umayyad dynasty, then by the 'Abbāsid. But locally the balance was otherwise in the shadow or on the margin of the 'Abbāsid dynasty; there were the régimes of vassal or independent principalities which gradually acquired an identity of their own in the peripheral regions; there was the régime of the Umayyad caliphate in Spain, the régime of the Būyid emirs which imposed itself for a century on the rulers of Baghdad, then the régime of the Seljuk sultans from 1045, to which were added, at the western extremity of the Islamic world, the Almoravid state, then the Almohad, not forgetting the non-Sunnite régimes which appeared here and there, sometimes in ephemeral fashion, sometimes in distant regions like the Yemen, sometimes too, at the very heart of the Islamic world where the flowering of the Fātimid dynasty enjoyed a long spring. Each of these régimes was in part the fruit of original politico-religious tendencies, following programmes more or less affirmed according to the case, but always clear to anyone examining the detail of the institutions in question.

In fact, governmental organisation properly called was not content to obey empirical rules in medieval Islam; it also rested on principles invoked in a way more or less explicit and it was in this sense the occasion for developments due to genuine theorists. Take, for example, what was accomplished in the Sunnite world of the eleventh century by the two great jurists al-Māwardi and Abū Ya'lā who, in spite of personal differences, wrote two treatises where they only disagreed on secondary points when describing the functions of the caliph as well as those of his various representatives, ministers, judges, emirs and administrators. This was an attempt at methodical justification where we find the bases of a complete account of the institutions then flourishing. In particular we learn that the caliph, the successor of the Prophet, charged with 'the upkeep of religion and the conduct of politics', had to observe a certain number of duties, such as fighting innovations in the religious domain, ensuring the execution of justice, applying legal penalties, assuring the internal security of Islamic territory and defending its frontiers, undertaking the holy war, receiving taxes and determining expenditure, in short, personally supervising the direction of affairs.

Such data could not but be amply utilised by orientalists to describe the classical institutions. We shall everywhere observe that neither did they take into consideration the slow development which took place during the centuries preceding the date of composition of the treatises thus made use of, nor the real conditions in which the power thus defined was often exercised. This is not to say that they were useless for the historian, but simply that they express an ideal situation, sometimes far removed from reality, and that they do not always make clear how the system came into being whose functioning the jurists in question were concerned to explain.

Thus it seems preferable to us to have recourse here to another approach and in our researches to give priority, apart from the writings of these eleventh century theorists, to what can be learnt from the facts themselves, which can be known from the writings of the historians, and which deserve therefore to be assessed in their relation to the corresponding currents of thought. It is true that such an examination has never before been undertaken in its entirety, but at least an attempt can be made to get some idea of its importance through a first series of observations. These will allow us to return to certain doctrinal questions which confronted the earliest Muslim community and more especially to envisage their effect on the ties which were then established between Islam and the political order.

I THE CONCEPTIONS OF POWER

The Koranic text, to which one would first be tempted to turn in order to discover the origin of these conceptions, does not in fact provide in this respect any precise definition, and justifies, by this very deficiency, the climate of constant discussion in which, in medieval Islam, the problem of power was always raised. The only verse that might be invoked is the one called 'the verse of the emirs', 'Obey God, His messenger and those in authority' (*ūlū l-amr*). It was a verse setting out a duty of obedience for the believer but showing no interest at all in the nature of the authority which he was thus urged to obey nor in the circumstances in which it appeared. At most, it may be inferred that political obedience is narrowly bound up with obedience to God, since an authority coming from God and from Him alone had been conferred in the first place on His Messenger, that is, on the one whose essential quality was to transmit the revealed message and himself to supervise the application of its precepts.

Thus if the organisation of the Islamic states in the Middle Ages was in some way ordered by Islam, the ideas which governed this organisation derived less from Koranic prescription than from an imitation of the attitude adopted by Muhammad himself when he had directed the Muslim community. This attitude inspired the attitude of his successors when they in their turn exercised authority. In other words, the foundation of this organisation was identified very soon with a tradition going back to the earliest times in Islamic history and concentrating on two essential questions: what sort of power had the Prophet of Islam exercised and to what extent had his immediate successors followed his example?

On the first point it is known that Muhammad, so long as he remained at Mecca, was content to proclaim a new religion and to behave as a preacher calling for conversion. Once he was installed at Medina with his followers, the situation changed completely and he had charge of a community which was temporal as well as spiritual. The community thus formed around him consisted of believers but also of Jews who recognised his authority, in particular his right to arbitrate in disputes which might arise between them. The existence of these non-Muslim elements moreover did not prevent the power of the Prophet being essentially of religious origin; if his arbitration was accepted by tribes not won over to Islam, it was because he had become the unquestioned head of a state of a type previously unknown where bonds of brotherhood had replaced traditional tribal ties.

For the rest, Muhammad, as we have seen during the years which followed, rarely failed to justify his deeds or his interventions by 'revelations' received at the opportune moment. All his important decisions concerning the direction of the community and the conduct of the military operations which he was led to undertake, as well as certain details of his private life, already mentioned, thus rested on instructions of divine origin. That is to say that his power was in fact theocratic in character, based essentially on the prophethood which the Muslims did not cease to acknowledge in him; all the later Muslim authors agree to see in him the *imām* par excellence, divinely inspired guide and master, who, even when he did not want to express a precise message, always acted with divine aid.

Nothing similar existed after his death when Abū Bakr, then 'Umar, then 'Uthmān and even 'Ali were, if not elected, properly speaking, at least chosen by the community of believers to be guides, in circumstances that were different and moreover not clearly defined. These persons, the 'rightly guided' caliphs, were indeed, as their title of *khalīfa* indicates, the 'successors' of the Prophet, but they did not themselves claim prophethood. It cannot always be said that they were purely temporal leaders for, if they were not charged to transmit a divine message, at least they had to preserve and apply that which Muhammad had previously delivered. Thus, as we have seen, they had to take decisions about the application of certain legal rules or of certain ritual prescriptions, then to interpret Islamic law and see that it was observed. They had to keep alive a custom formed in the time of Muhammad himself, under his inspiration or with his concurrence, and which played an essential role in establishing the Islamic order in its beginnings. Thus we can appreciate the importance of the problem which immediately presented itself and which was that of the conditions for assuming such a responsibility.

It was the effects of this problem, which appeared in the writings of the later theologians under the title of 'the problem of the imāmate' (each caliph being in his time the imām inheriting from Muhammad) which provoked most of the rivalries and armed struggles of the earliest Islamic history. It is true that we do not know exactly if, after the death of Muhammad, his son-in-law and cousin 'Ali had voiced claims to power because of his kinship with the deceased Prophet; but it has been seen how a party later came into being which upheld the rights of 'Ali against his three predecessors, who were accused of not having been really worthy of succeeding Muhammad.

The dissensions became more pointed under the reign of 'Uthmān, who belonged to an old Meccan family late in their conversion to Islam. He increased the resentment of his adversaries, when making appointments to governorships or lucrative posts, by calling on relatives judged competent in the matter of administration, because they were part of the great Arab merchants who had had long experience in business affairs. 'Ali, and his followers drawn from the Medinans who considered that belonging to the family of Muhammad conferred a pre-eminent right to direct the community, then rose up against these Meccans with even greater violence. The two concepts of power which confronted each other, having ended in the rifts of the first 'civil war' triggered off by the assassination of 'Uthmān, the victory of the defenders of the latter's cause, in this case the Banū Umayya, only drove back into opposition the movement favourable to the fourth caliph, who was henceforth deprived of his rights. From this came, at the heart of this Shi'ite party which itself later divided up into several branches, the adoption of a principle totally opposed to that recognised by the then ruling Umayyad caliphs, also opposed to that put forward by other partisans of 'Ali, who became secessionists and were known by the name of Khārijites, whose originality in some points of doctrine we have already indicated.

Three great concepts of power were thus defined in a more or less explicit fashion, from the beginning of the Umayyad period. The first of these wanted the caliphate to revert to 'Ali for two interconnected reasons, his kinship with the Prophet and also his early conversion to Islam. It also wanted the caliphate to revert to him so as to be transmitted afterwards to his descendants. Thus power remained the privilege of one family, that of Muhammad, in the heart of which discussions were aimed at selecting various privileged heirs, generally chosen from among the descendants of 'Ali and Fātima, the Prophet's daughter, that is, descendants of the Prophet himself through his daughter, although his kinship through the female line had not, in the early stages, been presented as the conclusive argument.

Another fundamentally opposed concept differed from this one, that of the Khārijites already mentioned, who became the adversaries of 'Ali while remaining the enemies of the caliph 'Uthmān. For the Khārijites the caliphate ought, on the contrary, to revert to the best member of the community without taking descent into account. In this case it was about an elected caliphate which could be equally temporary, since the caliph remained punishable by the possibility of deposition under the accusation of breach of the religious law.

Between these two positions there was the one which was defended by the Umayyad and 'Abbāsid caliphs, a position in which the rules chosen by the community undertook to lead it according to the principles of the Law and to defend its interests, without fear of ever being deposed, since the possibility of a condemnation aiming at his deposition was not foreseen. In this case, as also in the Khārijite position, the absence of any principle of dynastic succession meant that the caliphs strove to maintain the power of the members of their family by subterfuge and adopted the habit of designating as heir, during their life-time, the son or relative whom they themselves had chosen.

In a more general manner, the three concepts of power, which were thus differentiated by the Muslims of the first centuries, without impugning the Koranic message, but without exactly being inspired by it, corresponded in each case to a certain image of the ideal government. Among the Shi'ites, for example, as Montgomery Watt has emphasised, there was the image of the 'charismatic leader' belonging to a definite family and designated according to variable forms. For them the need was paramount to have a leader, visible or invisible, who had in some way received the spiritual heritage of the Prophet, who enjoyed divine assistance and committed neither fault nor error; even according to some of them, this leader could be called to deliver a new divine message which would complete or replace that transmitted by Muhammad.

It was on the contrary on the community itself, on the

totality of its members, that the Khārijites conferred these charismatic qualities. It was, according to them, the community which was seen to be infallible, and which, given this, was able to designate or depose a caliph, he being but the expression of their will.

Finally, in Sunnite circles, the charismatic idea never prevailed and never does one find the community having the power to proclaim the deposition of a caliph: the latter, once enthroned, could not be replaced by another. That at least was the opinion for which the first Umayyads tried to gain respect and which they succeeded in defending not without difficulty, in the midst of the diverse vicissitudes which marked their period of supremacy, namely, the revolt which had broken out under 'Uthmān and which ended with his assassination; the action of Mu'āwiya who had taken arms against 'Ali and had had arbiters appointed to find out whether 'Ali was worthy to rule or not, then saw to it that the arbitration ended in effect with the condemnation of 'Ali; the efforts of the governor of Mecca, Ibn al-Zubayr, to proclaim the deposition of the son and heir of 'Ali, at Kerbela. A little later, all the extraordinary energy of the Umayyad caliphs of the branch called Marwanid, in particular that of 'Abd al-Mālik, was needed to maintain an authority which had been breached in Arabia as well as in Iraq. From this came the propensity of all these rulers to act absolutely and to rely on the Murji'ite doctrine professed, as we have seen earlier, by certain scholars, according to which no one may judge the actions of another, no more those of the caliph than of any other believer.

In the same way, the caliph, in accordance with this Sunnite conception, was no longer able to lay claim to any superhuman quality. He was only chosen or accepted by the community to guide it, without however being seen to be either infallible or impeccable. It was only a quality of efficaciousness which was acknowledged in him. Nevertheless, this quality, once admitted officially, demanded obedience to him, since rebellion and schism were from that time on considered the worst evils that could befall a Muslim state.

Without doubt the experience of the first *fitna*, that which broke out after the murder of 'Uthmān, and the experience of the later civil wars which increased under the Umayyads, contributed to anchor this latter conviction. But we must also recognise that the Khārijite idea of the permanent control of the ruler by the community could not be realised in practice, especially from the moment the caliph did not present himself as a charismatic leader and when the unity of believers was no longer guaranteed except by a constant submission to his decisions.

In any case, the concept of power held by the Umayyads was defended anew by the 'Abbāsids who acceded to the caliphate in 750, and was justified chiefly in the course of the ninth century by the Hanbalite doctors. Indeed in this school it was claimed with considerable force that one must follow every imām, however wicked, in order to avoid splitting the community. The 'Murji'ite' belief which held that the believer could only be judged by God, was not explicitly spelt out in the professions of faith but none the less inspired them. This opinion was added to the idea of predetermination in order to form a doctrinal background according to which the fate of the individual was remitted to God as alone capable of assessing his degree of responsibility for his action; according to this background also, the community did not have authority to control the behaviour of the leader they had made and whose existence proved indispensable in applying the Law. What was required from this viewpoint was the cohesion of the religious group, where each attempted as best he could, while trusting in God but without being sure of succeeding, to be and to remain a 'believer'. For their part, the rulers, who were seen only as successors of the Prophet, were charged principally to keep the community on the right path, to defend it if need be, and to secure for each individual the possibility of observing the prescriptions of the religious law.

But if the Sunnite caliph thus held power by the agreement of the community to exercise it after the model of the Prophet, he was none the less considered to be the representative of God on earth and his title of *khalīfa* came to be interpreted in a sense which permitted him to demand almost unconditional submission. A single obligation devolved on him in return, as Ibn al-Muqaffa' clearly indicated when he was addressing the new 'Abbāsid caliph al-Mansūr, that of submitting himself to the religious Law and of not exercising his good pleasure except in the domain of 'government'.

Such a deepening of the Sunnite doctrine of the caliphate did not, however, sap the vitality of charismatic doctrines. The latter held their ground in the various branches of Shi'ism, chiefly in those of Imāmism and of Ismā'īlism whose beliefs, based on the recognition of a line of twelve or seven legitimate visible imāms, have been defined above. Ismā'īlism alone produced in the classical period an original political régime, that which was set up by the Fātimid dynasty first of Tunisia, then of Egypt, following the reappearance of a hidden imām, and which was then established on bases different from those which sustained Sunnite régimes: the Fātimid caliph ought never in principle to be either designated or accepted by the community but he was to be chosen by his predecessor who did this in secret fashion, and the believers were only then invited to obey him and swear allegiance to him. The fundamental difference thus proclaimed at the level of principles did not always show itself clearly in Fātimid practice which was very similar to that in vogue among the Sunnites from the Umayyad period onwards. What in fact happened was that a designation of a caliph, known only to a very highly placed dignitary close to the ruler, was contested on the death of the latter and this weakened the very basis of the régime. It also happened that a split in the community followed, as was the case with the succession to al-Mustansir, when the supporters of Nizār, who had been rejected by the majority of the dignitaries and the populace, founded a movement in favour of this claimant, called Nizarite or Neo-ismā'īli, which developed chiefly in Iran.

Similarly, another element characteristic of charismatic teaching does not appear to have been any more respected among the Fātimids, namely, the right allowed by this teaching to the ruler to interpret the Law, even to modify the message of Muhammad or to complete the first revelation. In this respect the Fātimid régime did not contrast sharply with the Umayyad and 'Abbāsid régimes. One of its caliphs, indeed, al-Hākim, allowed himself to be regarded by some of his followers as a veritable god, by a deflection of thought which Ismā'īli teaching helps to explain. But this was a unique incident and on the whole the Fātimid caliphs, although they regarded themselves as doctors, had recourse to specialists in law or theology when it came to defining official doctrine.

Above all, it was the Zaydite imāms, installed in the Yemen at the end of the ninth century and devoid of charismatic claims, who, strange to relate, proved themselves authentic scholars. They carried out erudite researches and participated actively in elaborating a doctrine which, as we have seen, modelled itself theologically on that of the Mu'tazilites. This fact is explained by the care with which these rulers had to be chosen, on the basis of their personal qualities, from among the descendants of 'Ali, according to a demand of their movement. It would seem that it was a formula of this kind that the 'Abbāsid caliph al-Ma'mūn wanted to adopt when, by his personal choice of a successor, he tried to transform the régime in existence until then. But his attempt failed, and any modification of the 'Abbāsid imāmate beyond the strict Sunnite concept was no longer possible.

2 Transmission and devolution of power

We have seen that the conflicting conceptions of power differed on the place which family descent should have in the designation of a new *imām*. Opposing the Shi'ite legitimism was the egalitarian spirit of the Khārijites. Between these two positions the Sunnite world had adopted a solution which, in principle, did not take account of birth, at least within the clan of Quraysh to which the Prophet had belonged, but which led to the possibility of a dynastic transmission of authority. And so began a policy of family continuity, not justified by any Koranic prescription nor by any prophetic tradition, but which could be practised without contradicting the custom of popular designation, in so far as taking the oath was always necessary before a caliph could effectively ascend the throne. In this way of proceeding, the approval of the community was reconciled with the maintenance of power by a single dynasty, and the foundation of sovereignty remained the contract agreed at the taking the oath or *bay'a* between each new sovereign and his subjects; this created obligations on both sides which it was in principle impossible to break although it remained permissible to make preparations in advance.

It was in fact the custom for the caliph to choose an heir to the throne (*walī al-'ahd*) whom he himself presented to his subjects, or at least to the most important among them, on the occasion of a ceremony similar to that which marked his own enthronement. We know that in the latter case the caliph – or his representative in the provinces – received the oaths to him taken by the inhabitants of the capital or of each principal town, after assembling inside the great mosque. The same rite, that of striking the hand of the prince as he sat on the *minbar*, was used to guarantee to the ruler's decision the popular confirmation which, from the beginning, was necessary at the time of the accession to the throne of each new caliph.

Certainly the forms changed little with time. The principal ceremony marking the actual enthronement was split into two parts: one took place at the palace, where the court dignitaries had just performed an act of allegiance, and this was the most important, since certain members of the 'aristocracy' and the caliph's entourage then solemnly declared that they recognised the authority of their new master; the other part took place in the great mosque, where as a rule the caliph no longer appeared himself but was represented by a delegate charged with receiving the oath of the people, a ceremony which was often fictitious but which always, in grave circumstances, recovered its whole meaning. Similarly, the announcement of the devolution of power to such and such a person of the ruling family might be made according to slightly different forms at each period; and one knows the example of the plan to divide up responsibilities between two of his sons, one as caliph, the other as governor of Khorasan, which was devised by Hārūn al-Rashīd, and to which he gave a sanction by placing a written will in the interior of the Ka'ba. But the desired object was always the same, that of legalising, by the guaranteed agreement of the community, a devolution of power which corresponded to personal and family ambitions.

The system thus adopted did not, however, hinder dynastic aspirations, in the course of centuries, from coming up against many difficulties and these make it easier to understand certain aspects of political organisation. We already know that after the earliest discussions, those which led after Muhammad's death to the prevention of representatives of the Medinan faction from being elected to the caliphate, the Umayyad family had in practice taken possession of the power and made it its own property. We also know that this family succeeded in preserving and even increasing its authority after the crisis following on the death of the grandson of Mu'āwiya. If the Umayyads managed to get respect on the whole for a legitimism based on the fact that their ancestors formed the most important element in the Quraysh clan, they were not able, however, to determine the principle regulating each caliph's choice of successor, so that lawsuits were always liable to arise on the death of a ruler who, during his lifetime, had not taken the necessary steps to see that his son succeeded him.

The situation was similar under the 'Abbāsids, who also claimed to be the heirs of a power regarded as personal property. In their turn they had to establish their own legitimism, relying this time on their membership of the Prophet's family, but in a perspective which had nothing in common with the one which was the basis of the claims of the 'Alids: indeed they were content to recall the Koranic prescriptions which, regarding inheritance, gave preference to the uncle, in this case their own ancestor al-'Abbās, to the detriment of the daughter, in this case Fātima, wife of 'Ali. On this basis it was possible for them to keep the choice of caliph within the 'Abbāsid family, but they were forced, like the Umayyads, to rest their concern for dynastic continuity on the official recognition, by the community, of each heir designated by the ruling sovereign. The same oppositions between claimants and the same disputes as in the preceding epoch thus showed themselves for the same reasons; no prior order of succession within the caliph's family was in fact specified and if the majority of rulers chose as heir their son or one of their sons, who was not necessarily the eldest, we see how, on several occasions, a brother or a cousin would contest the decision by virtue of an ancient customary right. These lawsuits became even more acute in the case where a ruler died without designating an heir, all the more so because the age of majority demanded for accession to the throne was not fixed in a precise manner.

Other solutions prevailed later among families, generally non-Arab, who seized actual authority from the beginning of the tenth century in more or less extensive regions of the medieval Islamic world, legitimising themselves as recipients of powers delegated by a caliph of diminished authority. Among the Būyids of Iranian origin as among the Seljuks of Turkish origin or the Ayyūbids of Kurdish origin, power was held to be a family possession which could possibly give rise to a division. This explains the frequent rivalries which arose between brothers or between cousins or between uncle and nephew, ending up more often than not with a division of the kingdom, but sometimes also leading one of the claimants to make the others recognise his authority and thus to re-establish temporarily the unity of the territory.

Thus it was with the Būyids who were almost constantly at war with one another. So too, with the Seljuks, where however we find various situations. The first sultans held power from father to son, with the exception of Tughril Beg who succeeded his brother and was then replaced by his nephew; the sons of the third 'great Seljuk', Malikshāh, later disputed between themselves about the empire, while their uncle set himself up in Syria, where he was to leave power to his two sons, who divided up the principality between them. There was also a brother of the second sultan, Alp Arslān, who took possession of the Iranian province of

Kirman where he founded his own dynasty. A little later, among the Ayyūbids, the successors of Saladin, the most serious rivalry arose between the son of the founder of the dynasty and his uncle, al-Malik al-'Adil, who reigned over Egypt and southern Syria while the son had to be content with the region of Aleppo.

We can moreover observe that similar problems arose in the Berber states of the Maghrib. Among the Almohads, especially, power was at first in the hands of the 'Mahdi' Ibn Tumart, who ruled with the help of a small number of faithful companions from whom was chosen his successor, 'Abd al-Mu'min. It then reverted to this latter to appropriate, as it were, the government of the kingdom thus constituted, and to found a hereditary dynasty, that of the Mu'minids: dynastic practice was once more substituted for the primitive system, following a process which recalled what had happened in the early days of Islam.

Thus in all the different states, whether ruled by caliphs, sultans or emirs, a dynastic transfer of power nearly always came into being, but the absence of a rule of succession allowed certain customs of tribal origin to oppose the proclivity of rulers in general to bequeath power to one of their sons. Besides, the collective conception of power which appeared in some emirs' families, only served to increase an instability already frequent in caliphal régimes. This instability, which counterbalanced to a certain extent the despotic nature of power, was an important characteristic of political life; it aroused the disenchanted reflections of an Ibn Khaldūn who considered dynasties and states as bound to the laws of biological development, while current Muslim mentality saw in it the effects of blows of fate willed by the Almighty.

3 The exercise of power in the Sunnite world

Bound up with the conceptions of power are not only the modes of transfer of authority but also the conditions for exercising this power which we know especially, as far as the medieval Islamic world is concerned, in the Sunnite framework of the 'Abbāsid caliphate. The distinction already made in this respect by Ibn al-Muqaffa' between the sphere of religion and that of government, a distinction whose apparent logic cannot be denied, would make one think that the 'Abbāsid caliph, ruling over so vast an empire, never had any independence except in those affairs beyond the reach of the Law; he himself had to submit to the Law and could not deviate from it since he was specially charged with safeguarding it.

In fact the reality was not as simple, and, from the earliest times, this problem of relations between the caliph and the Law and of relations between the caliph and men of religion presented itself in terms liable to enhance, there also, the extent of the caliph's power. This situation was at first connected with the circumstances in which Islamic Law itself had gradually taken shape, beginning with Koranic prescriptions or affirmations which were sometimes rudimentary, laconic or ambiguous; it had very soon been necessary, even in a Sunnite Muslim environment, to know if the Prophet's heir, the guardian of the Law, should not also intervene in the modes of its application.

To the question thus raised, the response, if one believes sound traditions, was at first positive, since the caliphs had to take decisions of a legal nature in those cases where the text of the revelation was not sufficiently explicit. It appears that later the cadis replaced them in this task, and took the initiative of legislating in the regions where they found themselves, without referring to the governor or the ruler, while the jurists, for their part, undertook to define the practical rules, which as a whole were gradually integrated into the very body of the Law: thus magistrates and doctors acted and worked in an independent fashion to the point of arousing, at the beginning of the 'Abbāsid epoch, the disquiet echoed by Ibn al-Muqaffa' and which led him to approach the caliph to suggest a unification of the customs in use and to promulgate a code which could apply throughout the Empire.

The programme thus suggested not only constituted an important initiative on the legal plane at a time when a doctrine, whose slow maturing we have already mentioned, was also being defined through discussions and conflicts; it also made the ruler face his responsibilities in his relations with the Law. The wise reaction of the caliph al-Mansūr, who refused to act as requested, influenced the future, by leaving to the free decision of the cadis everything concerning private life, social relations, ritual and worship, while the caliph reserved for himself only the right to decide in contentious cases where he appeared as the supreme arbiter.

However, his attitude was different on administrative questions, notably the tax system which had a direct effect on state finances and which was efficiently organised by the early rulers. In fact originally the community revenues were of two kinds: the sum of the legal alms paid by Muslims on their goods (herds, crops) and that of a booty which increased with the extension of the territories conquered by force. The booty was shared among the combatants according to precise rules, but when it came to land, it was customary to leave the use of it to its old occupants in return for payment of a tax which was considered as rent for land which had become, as such, the property of the Muslim community. A fiscal system was thus set up and defined by the theoreticians from the eighth century, and established gradually by the Umayyad caliphs by adapting Koranic principles to the previous practices of the subject populations and by getting round, by appropriate measures, the successive difficulties which occupation and conversion soon caused to appear.

We know, for example, that at the end of the Umayyad period the converted farmers, who had become more and more numerous, began to desert their lands in order to settle in the large towns; they estimated that once they became Muslims, they had only to pay a tax equivalent to that paid by the Arabs, that is, a tithe on their harvests corresponding to the legal alms, and in consequence tried to get rid of their old obligations by flight; the migration soon took on such proportions that, because the lands were no longer cultivated, the taxes were no longer paid and the treasury suffered. It was then that caliph ʻUmar II issued a famous rescript which, to satisfy those complaining, allowed their residence in the towns, but which prohibited the extension of the movement and kept the land tax attached to the land, while it seems, dissociating it from the personal tax due from non-Muslims; the convert was nevertheless exonerated in part from the fiscal charge, which weighed heavily on him, and, in addition, the non-Muslim was no longer subjected as before to the global tax levied on the whole of a village community. Two land taxes found themselves thus defined, the tithe (*'ushr*) imposed on the revenue from the ancient lands possessed by the Muslims, and the *kharāj*, which still applied to all conquered territories whatever the religion of the farmers, and which clearly amounted to more than the tithe.

Such a reform, whose application was however called in question, was certainly of importance. But the establishing of rules of this kind for the collection of tax did not limit the action of the caliphs, who did not cease to act in things fiscal. They were always at liberty to modify the status of a given piece of land, in particular to reduce the rate of tax. They could also grant dispensations or reductions. Above all, they alone could distribute 'land concessions', which at first included the lands whose owners had fled at the conquest and which had been handed over for the time being to the principal conquering Arab leaders, who were authorised to exploit them by paying only the lesser tax of the tithe. This system had been widely used in regions like Syria by the Umayyad caliphs, who had been thus able to set up their army there and to provide its officers with substantial revenues. It was kept on by the 'Abbāsid caliphs for the benefit of the leaders of their new troops of mercenaries or for the benefit of various court dignitaries. But however the system functioned then, it had no effect on the revenues from tax. On the contrary the latter decreased in the tenth century when the Būyid emirs, who then held power along with a declining 'Abbāsid caliphate decided to distribute new land concessions from now on liable to the tithe on lands, subject until then to *kharāj*. The operation, which was disastrous for the treasury, required a modification of the status of the lands thus utilised; it could only be done with the agreement of the caliph and by reason of the rights which he reserved to himself. This operation was none the less repeated afterwards, in particular in the period of the Seljuk sultans, who wanted to give their military leaders similar advantages guaranteed by land concessions, and who continued to modify in depth the fiscal organisation of the Empire.

Thus, although the caliph might at first be the simple 'guide' of Muslims in the line traced by the Prophet, he preserved in practice a freedom of action which had profound consequences. This liberty too was so much the greater that it often proved difficult, if not impossible, for any one to distinguish between modes of application and modifications of the very principles of the Law. The duty of 'holy' or legal war (*jihād*) for which the caliph assumed special responsibility deserves in this connection to be taken as an example: if the ruler could not modify the principle, it was at least for him alone to define its observance, that is, to decide when it was the right moment to set out on an expedition against infidel territory, or again to rule on when it was a question of concluding a truce or proceeding to ransom prisoners. In the same way, the caliph, given charge of arranging the annual Pilgrimage, reserved among his prerogatives whether himself to lead the caravan which travelled to Mecca by routes which were not always very safe, or whether to appoint a member of his family or entourage to fulfil this function, which demanded real organisational qualities.

It should be added that the caliph possessed equally extended powers in judicial matters. Doubtless he normally delegated their exercise to magistrates, the cadis, who while following legal prescriptions, also took into account the customs of each region, and had also, in settling most litigation, to depend on their personal opinion and on their own sense of equity. But the decisions taken by this or that cadi in the wide field of action open to him, namely that of penal jurisdiction, of civil jurisdiction and of the application of personal status in the matter of marriage and succession could not remain without appeal. The caliph was in this case the supreme arbiter to whom one could have recourse directly or through the intermediacy of his representatives when one wished to quash a judicial decision which appeared unjust. He was *par excellence* the 'redresser of wrongs', and normally received – or arranged to have received – each week the plaintiffs who were not satisfied with the way their affairs had been settled. It was the special jurisdiction of the 'redressing of wrongs' at which ended up also all the complaints relative to the administrative decisions of the central government or of its provincial representatives.

We must further remember that the caliph had the upper hand over the police who were charged on the one hand to carry out sentences promulgated by the cadis in penal matters, such as chastising thieves, and on the other hand to ensure the maintenance of order by means of sanctions and punishments not provided for by Koranic legislation, but corresponding to the needs of the time. This role of a police force, which depended directly on the ruler and which gave him every facility to exercise his arbitrary decision, could still be increased on occasion and extend to the entire domain of penal justice, thus taken away from the authority of the cadis. So the caliph who thus had at his command a prefect of police who was sometimes very powerful, also exercised his power through the person of the *muhtasahib*, this 'provost' charged with control of the markets, with suppressing fraud, with watching over morals and opinions, in general with imposing on urban society what might be called the Islamic moral order.

But what is even more important is that the caliph, who was charged, by virtue of his function as guardian of religion, with suppressing dangerous innovations, with combating what we would call heresy and with keeping the community on the right road, came to intervene in the realm of doctrine, without however exercising a true magisterium since he did not take the role of doctor. On several occasions it thus happened that certain 'Abbāsid rulers recommended, if not imposed, a somewhat novel religious trend. It is this which explains the changes which came about, firstly at the beginning of the ninth century when al-Ma'mūn chose to impose the Mu'tazilite doctrine on all those who exercised a judicial function, secondly at the beginning of the tenth century when the traditionalist Hanbalite doctrine was condemned, and thirdly at the beginning of the eleventh century when this same doctrine was on the contrary solemnly adopted by the caliph al-Qādir in an effort to combat the influence of the Būyid emirs with Shi'ite sympathies. It is true that, in these different cases, a relative freedom of opinion was respected within the population. But the condemned doctrines could no longer be made the object of public teaching, and such a prohibition shows the extent of the caliph's influence in religious matters, which has sometimes been misunderstood.

By virtue of the same principle authorising him to suppress all doctrinal deviation, the caliph had equally the duty to tackle rebellions which called into question the positions which he and the principal doctors had determined. In this capacity it fell to him to interrogate, assisted by cadis and doctors, the heretics or the blasphemers who had fallen into the hands of the police, and, on the other hand, to direct military operations against the rebels, who were always followers of a doctrine opposed to the official doctrine, as well as being at the same time opponents of the régime. There was indeed hardly an example, in the 'Abbāsid period, of a sizeable revolt which had not been launched in the name of some heresy, and which did not depend on some sectarian movement. Even when apparently dealing with a personal dynastic quarrel, different politico-religious conceptions appeared in the background, as happened for example at the beginning of the ninth century during the civil war between al-Ma'mūn and his brother al-Amīn, the two sons of Hārūn al-Rashīd: one of the two protagonists held in fact to a traditionalist interpretation of Islam while the other was attracted by the rationalist tendency of the Mu'tazilite theologians.

It resulted from this situation that, during the whole 'Abbāsid period, the defence of the established régime and of the dynasty bound to this régime was identified with the defence of the Muslim community, and this left the caliph free in punishing the enemies of the dynasty to use all the means legally at his disposal and to suppress, as he understood it, the attacks directed through him against Islam. Thus he had all power, beginning with the right of life and death, over those who showed some opposition to him, not only external enemies and armed rebels but also dignitaries or ministers who followed a policy not in line with the one he desired or who hindered the realisation of his own objectives. By means of this repressive power he was able to appear as a truly autocratic ruler.

It is, however, clear that this caliphal autocracy needed, in order to function, the support of what might be called the large bodies of state, even if the expression does not convey exactly the situation in the Islamic world. The arbitrary ruler was not in fact able to go beyond certain limits without raising the protestations of court dignitaries or even in certain extreme cases of the 'doctors' or of public opinion. The caliph was no more able to govern without the active assistance of military leaders who sometimes plotted to overthrow him, that is, to assassinate him or to constrain him to abdicate, since there was no legal procedure provided in Sunnism for his deposition. Thus we see in the period when the 'Abbāsid caliphs resided at Samarra (836–83) the Turkish chiefs 'making and unmaking' caliphs whom they sometimes deposed for purely personal reasons. We see still later, after the caliphs had succeeded in controlling their Turkish guard more effectively, conspiracies flourishing which brought together a mixture of people and which led to palace revolutions, sometimes crowned with success, sometimes ephemeral, as under al-Muqtadir. Participating in these conspiracies were not only officers and palace guards but also viziers and secretaries of state when these latter had succeeded in acquiring an influence which would allow them to appear as masters of the situation. The role which devolved on members of the administration was however rarely decisive, as is illustrated by the powerlessness of the vizier 'Ali b. 'Isā to get the deposition of the caliph al-Qāhir proclaimed in 934; and the same comment is valid for the cadis and other men of religion who in general disliked getting involved in acts of this sort.

The doctors, when they disapproved of the caliph's policy, more and more practised a form of passive resistance, which was particularly successful in the period when the caliph al-Ma'mūn wanted to give the 'Abbāsid régime a Mu'tazilite orientation. Indeed it was not then possible for the traditionalists, who refused this initiative on the part of the ruler, to make him abdicate. But the firmness shown by them in the face of power pressures, menaces and ill-treatment, makes them seem like martyrs for holding to their faith or at least to their inner convictions, and the prestige they gained in the eyes of public opinion forced the successors of al-Ma'mūn in the course of time to abandon his policy in order to take account of this latent opposition.

Moreover it should be noted that in certain other cases violent popular riots could force caliphs to revoke a decision they had taken. Thus, when the same al-Ma'mūn chose as heir an 'Alid prince not belonging to the 'Abbāsid family his decision caused a revolt among the inhabitants of Baghdad and even of Iraq, and that was enough, when he was told about it – for he was then residing in eastern Iraq – to make him abandon this project.

4 The organisation of government

The quasi-despotic powers of the Sunnite 'Abbāsid caliph could only be exercised in so far as his entourage and public opinion allowed. Moreover he did not rule alone but by means of a cumbersome administrative system concentrated at the heart of the empire and by the intermediacy of representatives who were his delegates both for the control of the central services and those of the distant regions and who held from him alone an authority sometimes subject to variations.

The form of government of the provinces did not, for example, cease to change constantly from the first attempts at unifying the empire, and it remained one of the weakest points of the medieval Islamic system. In the earliest period the responsibilities were combined in the hands of the governor, the military leader on whom depended the activities of the tax collector, and who himself nominated the judges. The 'Abbāsid caliphs wanted to remedy this situation, which persisted during the Umayyad period, by managing, at least in the beginning, to substitute for it a more centralised administration. Thus they limited the powers of the governors, dangerous because they controlled the military force, and they (the caliphs) reserved for themselves not only the nomination of the tax collectors but also that of the cadis; and when the central office of the great cadi had been created the caliphs then had the post filled through him. From then on the authority of the caliph was assured in the provinces by the reciprocal independence of three people who were his delegates – the emir or military governor, the tax collector and the judge.

Normally the provincial director of finances deducted from the locally collected taxes the sum needed for the expenses of the province, especially the upkeep of troops stationed in the territory, and only sent the surplus to the treasury. But the whole of these operations came within the competence of the central services. It needed exceptional circumstances accompanied by financial difficulties before the ruler would concede the farming of taxes to some individual, that is, the responsibility of collecting the taxes in exchange for the immediate payment to the treasury of a fixed sum which had afterwards to be recovered from the taxpayers; the sum of the concession was generally less than the real sum of the taxes and it was in fact known that the caliph's government was losing, in the course of such an operation, a part of its normal revenues.

With time, however, the exceptional practice became the rule, although the balance reached one moment declined the next and although the 'tax farmers' in ever-increasing numbers took advantage of the need of money by caliph and court to hold the latter at the mercy of their demands. Various provinces of the empire had in fact escaped progressively from 'Abbāsid domination, and the resources of central government had been accordingly reduced. After the western regions (Spain, the far Maghrib, Ifriqiya) had broken away in the course of the eighth century, Egypt and Khurasan had, in practice, towards the middle of the ninth century followed the same path: the governors who had been appointed there became hereditary dynasties, content to pay modest tribute to the caliph who, in some cases, waged costly military operations against them in vain. Thus it was that the rulers of Baghdad, perpetually short of cash, had, at the beginning of the tenth century, to authorise certain governors of western Iran or lower Iraq themselves to fill the functions of 'tax farmers'. These functions gave to some individuals an increased power and finally allowed them to get the better of the caliph; in 936 al-Rādi found himself obliged to abandon all his powers, military and financial, to a 'grand emir', who from now on governed the empire or at least what remained of it.

But the relations between the provinces were not alone in necessitating the use by the caliph of auxiliaries more or less efficient but more or less greedy for power. There also existed around the ruler a complex administrative organisation, which had gradually grown up since the time of the Umayyad dynasty, but which always presented a mobility reflecting the actual condition in which the autocratic power of the caliph was exercised. The respective spheres of the various individuals determined by the holder of supreme authority, in fact only depended on his arbitrary will in the measure that these administrators at first appeared as servants of the caliph who embodied the state. Thus personal ties often existed between the ruler and the 'senior civil servants' who were admitted to exercise responsibility in the government as well as to administer this or that specialised service, the most important role among them being devolved upon the vizier, whose title and function grew progressively at the beginning of the 'Abbāsid period.

The Umayyad caliphs were in fact content to take into their service secretaries to whom they left little initiative except perhaps during the last period of the dynasty's existence. The first 'Abbāsid caliphs, on the other hand, wanted to utilise extensively the abilities of those individuals serving them as auxiliaries. Adopting, it seems, a usage which had been common in revolutionary Shi'ite circles where they themselves had found help and support, they had recourse to the term of *wazīr* to describe one of these auxiliaries, a term which had designated in such circles the 'chief propagandist', the 'authorised representative', in a fashion, of the claimant. Nevertheless they used this appellation in another context, and following the reference in the Koran which describes Hārūn/Aaron as *wazīr* of Mūsā/Moses, they applied it to those of their secretaries to whom they had entrusted important responsibilities associated with the service of their own person. A title so charged with religious value, used equally in the past by the Arab historians to designate the ministers of the great Sassanid king, could only heighten the prestige of the ruler who awarded it, and who sought, in naming a *wazīr*, to appear at one and the same time emulator of a Biblical prophet helped by God and also as the equal of the King of Kings.

In fact it was only from the middle of the ninth century that the caliphs nominated viziers in a regular way. Before that, the 'Abbāsids in power had mostly preferred a close personal direction of government policy. Only some among them had felt the need to confer this exceptional title on people of different origins, some of whom acted as secretaries for lands and specialists in finance, others as confidants of the ruler, without always having any precise qualification. Afterwards the vizier had to combine such diverse qualities as those of administrative expert and those of confidential adviser of the caliph in order to play his double role, transmitting on the one hand the prince's orders to various administrative heads, and conducting on the other hand the general policy according to directives which his master gave him, without wishing himself to verify the detail of their execution.

Thus the viziers of the first period had in general, when the post existed, only few personal responsibilities. Only one exception must be made, towards the end of the eighth century, for the famous Barmakids, a father and his two sons, who were ministers of Hārūn al-Rashīd but of whom we do not know exactly which bore the title of *wazīr*.

Yahyā, the father, was a secretary with wide experience of financial affairs. He and his sons, without taking precedence over one another, were the assistants and intimates of the caliph, who eventually charged them with more precise tasks: thus to al-Fadl fell the task of suppressing the rebellion of an 'Alid in Tabaristan, while a little later his brother Ja'far was sent to Syria to calm the troubles there. Thus they were not simply administrators but delegates who could be invested with military commands. The powers which they enjoyed officially nevertheless appear to have been always limited, and, if Arab historians have been able to speak of the 'dictatorship' or at least of the 'reign of the Barmakids', the term could not make people forget that these latter always performed their activities under the control of a caliph, who did not hesitate, in the moment of their famous disgrace, violently and without appeal, to relieve himself of them: their power, fragile for all that, thus depended less on their functions than on the influence which they had managed to acquire temporarily with a master whose favourite counsellors they were. Immediately after them, the office of vizier was filled by mediocre individuals, outstanding among whom stood out the minister of al-Ma'mūn, the Iranian al-Fadl ibn Sahl, who dominated his master for several years and, it seems, by his determination, enabled him to gain victory over his half-brother al-Amīn, one-time caliph in Iraq.

But the situation changed completely towards the end of the ninth century when we see the vizier occupying alongside the emir, who was the commander in chief, and the grand cadi, a real position of prime minister, co-ordinating administrative activities and participating in the formulation of general policy, including military policy. The holders of this post, then officially recognised, were more than ever chosen from among financial specialists, since the financial problem began to form the chief preoccupation of the 'Abbāsid government after the exceptional expense caused by the various rebellions which had arisen even in Iraq. These viziers, though financiers, were no less concerned with other questions, and acted by means of politico-religious choices corresponding to the opinions of the rival clans to which they belonged; we know that each of them, when he was nominated, brought with him his working team, all of them people whose first care was to profit from the situation and to inflict penalties on their predecessors, who were inevitably accused of misappropriation. We must recognise moreover that honesty hardly prevailed among the senior civil servants; for the most part they only dreamed of making themselves rich at the expense of a ruler whose legitimacy some went so far as to contest in their heart of hearts, for the caliph was sometimes led to choose his vizier from circles favourable to Shi'ism.

This 'triumph of the vizier' was only of short duration, however, before the rise of the military leaders. It is true that his function was retained in the East, even after the appearance of the grand emir, then of the sultan. But the caliph's vizier, reduced to the function of personal secretary, no longer played any political role until the period in the course of the twelfth century when his master succeeded in recovering a part of his pre-eminence, while the emirs or sultans each had, at their service, their own vizier also assuming important responsibilities.

Furthermore, in Muslim Spain there also existed at the time of the emirate, then of the caliphate, a post of prime minister given to individuals who indeed bore another title, that of chamberlain or *ḥājib* but who exercised prerogatives similar to those of the vizier in the East, while the name of *wazīr* was in this province conferred on the principal counsellors of the realm. As to the Fāṭimid régime, it also had viziers as 'prime ministers' who in the later period, exercised military as well as political powers, allowing them to substitute their authority completely for that of a ruler now held in tutelage.

In 'Abbāsid Iraq, where this final step of evolution is not encountered, and where the viziers never attained the same independence or power, the caliph none the less ceased to be a ruler in the full sense of the term from the middle of the tenth century. His powers were then delegated first to the 'grand emirs' who governed from 936 to 1055, then to 'sultans' who succeeded them. If the earlier all-powerful leaders of the community kept (at the time of the 'grand emirs' who became in 945 Shi'ite emirs) some prerogatives, it was no longer the same in the time of the Seljuk sultans who presented themselves as the defenders of Sunnite Islam and whose orthodoxy was not suspect to the caliphs. At first the Seljuks were sole sultans and sole delegates with caliphal powers, but later had rapidly to share this privilege with others; there were in the 'Abbāsid empire several sultans, who each had authority over a particular region.

This was the recognition of a political splitting-up whose effects had for long been felt in the West, where the authority of the 'Abbāsid caliph, already rejected in the ninth century by the emirs of the Umayyad family installed in Muslim Spain as well as by certain dynasties of the Maghrib, had been finally challenged in 929. In that year the emir 'Abd al-Rahmān had taken the title of caliph to defend Sunnism simultaneously against the pretensions of the Fātimid caliphate, which had recently appeared, and against the dangers which in the East threatened a caliphate itself struggling with ambitious military leaders. The disappearance a little later, at the beginning of the eleventh century of this caliphate of Cordova made room for numerous petty rulers, while in the Maghrib the Fātimids were replaced by Sunnite dynasties, at first Zīrids and others, then Almoravids and Almohads. But in practice nothing had changed in the situation, even if the various states progressively came to recognise the theoretical suzerainty of the caliph of Baghdad. Thus, and in spite of changing situations which brought back to him peripheral regions which had formerly seceded, the former master of the empire had at his disposal in the eleventh and twelfth centuries only a relative authority. If he remained the unique source of power, this power could be handed over to numerous princes bearing the title of sultan or sometimes only of emir. Each of these princes handed on the power thus acquired to his descendants, as had already been done for a long time by the governors claiming independence and founding local dynasties in each region by this expedient; this however did not prevent other officers from eventually seizing the said power and in turn founding new principalities.

To the power thus established in fact in each regional or local centre, its holder in any case tried generally, but not necessarily, to give a caliphal legitimisation which alone allowed him to justify legally the attributes of sovereignty which he had in his possession.

Everywhere, in fact, the splintered authority which ruled the Sunnite community now rested on force of arms rather than on free choice and in consequence the jurists had to modify certain of their theories. After al-Ghazāli, who thought that a man holding 'power and influence' – that is, the sultan – could designate the caliph, we see in the period which followed the Mongol invasions an Ibn Taymiyya reopen the whole question of the old conceptions of the imāmate, the bases of 'Abbāsid authority, in order to accept, in a certain measure, the devolving of power to whomever had in fact laid hold on it. The first Sunnite legitimism, once shattered by the Mongol invasion in 1260 had hardly any longer a zealous defender save the Mamluke sultans who had found it advantageous to give shelter at Cairo to descendants of the caliphal family to increase their prestige thanks to these. Then the idea spread, especially in the Turkish and Iranian regions, that every established ruler who respected Islamic law and saw that it was observed, deserved the epithet of 'caliph' and this could in one sense point to the later claim of the Ottoman sultans to possess the caliphate.

5 Prestige and ceremonial

This authority of absolute and quasi-despotic character exercised by every possessor of a throne in Islamic countries, thanks to the prescriptions but also to the silences of the Law, falls within the series illustrated by the great oriental monarchies, more particularly the Iranian. We have seen that certain measures taken by the 'Abbāsid caliphs, for example the nomination of 'viziers', tended to draw them closer both to the Prophet whose successors they were, and to the ancient kings of Persia. It will naturally always be difficult to estimate the part played by these influences, but it cannot be disputed that for a long time in the East the Sassanid example remained present to the spirit of the Muslim rulers. Some among them, like the Būyid emirs of Iranian origin, insisted moreover very particularly on the bonds linking them to the ancient dynasties of Iran.

In such a climate the arbitrary will of the prince was in each case reinforced by numerous measures destined to heighten his majesty, or that of his representatives, both with the courtiers and with the crowd. Their public life, and more particularly the caliph's, a model copied afterwards by everyone, was regulated by a minute etiquette, whose origin unquestionably reached back to a period before Islam. The ruler, who only appeared in public in clearly defined conditions, lived the rest of his time hidden in his palace. If he had to receive visitors or friends, the latter did not have free access to him and could only see him after having been introduced by the chamberlain (*hājib*), an individual who, because of this, played an essential role in the palace.

In the early days the 'Abbāsid caliph received homage each day from the courtiers but he did not appear before them and remained concealed behind a curtain; only certain individuals with whom he wanted to converse had official access to him. Later, audiences took place twice a week; dignitaries and courtiers were present occupying places assigned to them by virtue of their rank and also of their origin: admitted to these were important visitors, viziers or governors whom the caliph was investing, generals to whom he gave distinctions, and sometimes ambassadors from foreign countries. It was at these gatherings that sumptuous 'robes of honour' made in the caliph's workshops were distributed; some examples of these have been preserved and are one of the best testimonies of the artistic refinements of the period.

At the beginning of the tenth century the caliph sat on a large throne-divan, surrounded by his personal guard, covered with the Prophet's cloak, and wearing on his hand a ring, said to be that of the Prophet, which was in fact the chief insignia of his sovereignty; he also held in his left hand, a copy of the Koran of 'Uthmān which emphasised his role as guardian of orthodoxy. But this heir of Muhammad appeared above all as an Eastern monarch. During audiences, the curtain behind which he stood was only lifted when the visitor entered and the latter had immediately to prostrate himself and kiss the ground, a gesture he had to repeat several times before reaching the caliph. For their part, emirs and sultans giving audience in their own palaces as 'delegates' of the caliph, did not possess the same insignia but applied rules of ceremonial nearly identical.

The caliph's departures were regulated in the same way and only took place in defined circumstances. In the period of Samarra in the ninth century, the caliph rode solemnly out of his palace to lead the Friday Prayers in the great mosque; he was accompanied by a military escort, preceded by the chief of police carrying the lance said to have belonged to the Prophet and which was a symbol of sovereignty. In the tenth century the caliph was no longer needed to leave the residential complex to go to the great mosque, practically never appeared in public, while in Cairo the Fātimid caliph had adopted similar habits, only going out rarely for the Friday Prayers and for the celebration of certain great festivals. The ruler also had to review the troops whose nominal leader he was. But this custom is attested above all for the emirs who ruled in the twelfth century in Syria: for example, Nūr al-Dīn appeared then in a loggia fitted up specially in the palace of the citadel and looking down on the esplanade where the soldiers manoeuvred.

Thus surrounded by a luxury and a respect which isolated him, the medieval Islamic ruler, whether he was caliph, sultan or emir, remained difficult of access and acted as a veritable despot, despite attempts on the part of the lawyers to regulate the often exorbitant powers which he had assumed. Indeed he always appeared, before public opinion and before the doctors, as the worthy leader of a Muslim community – or of a fraction of a community – whose role remained primary. But his behaviour was that of an oriental monarch, as is attested at the height of the Islamic period by the numerous 'mirrors of princes' of Iranian inspiration, composed for his benefit and giving him many counsels, together with wise advice for this courtiers; for kings, in fact, the authors of these treatises recommended that they should know how to manage themselves, to reflect on the consequences of their actions, possibly to fear God, while of the courtiers they asked that they should learn how to avoid the wrath of their master and how to guide him usefully without however displeasing him. Through these works, as also through a number of anecdotes, the image of an irascible and capricious despot impresses itself on us, at the same time charged with magnificence and quite different from the image preserved in the treatises of public law. Doubtless it was still this image that ranked first for the contemporaries and which insured the brilliance of an office which no precise rule could hinder – at least at a certain period – from conquering by force, an image which consequently allowed an understanding of the place which personal or family political ambitions always held in the history of medieval Islam.

CHAPTER 5
Islam and the social order

Unlike the political order, the social organisation of Islamic countries in the Middle Ages was based partly on precise Koranic prescriptions, although it is not easier to characterise it in an overall manner. Contrary tendencies did not however cease to make themselves felt in the course of time, tendencies which coloured it in a different way according to the places and the periods, and which until recently have claimed insufficient attention. More particularly the problem of the hierarchies is one of those rarely touched on by orientalists except from the slightly different angle of social 'classes'. It would seem, however, that some contemporary comments, however brief, on this neglected question might provide us with the first steps towards a useful method of approach.

1 Egalitarianism and privileges in early times

The community which came into being after the proclamation of Muhammad's message, and which we know chiefly in its Umayyad form, presents in fact an ambiguous character. On the one hand, Islam asserts the quality of all Muslims, further reinforced by the fundamental differentiation which it made between Muslims and non-Muslims. On the other hand, the community which based itself on this new religious allegiance had hardly any respect for the principles of a strictly egalitarian organisation.

On the first point there should not be any doubt when we refer to the text itself of the Koran. Those who obey the call are distinguished from others who themselves belong moreover to two categories. The 'people of the Book', Christians and Jews, together with the Zoroastrians, enjoyed a protection which however could always be put in question if they did not give proof of the necessary loyalty; this explains the massacre of the Banū Qurayza, Jews of Medina, executed by order of the Prophet, and it also explains the reactions of those victims at the time of the Crusades, the Christians of Syria and still later the Christians of other regions, each time an Islamic country entered into armed conflict with a 'Christian' power. Faced with these 'protected' non-Muslims, equality should have prevailed among believers whatever their origin. This, as we have seen, is what Muhammad had recommended in his 'Farewell Address'.

But in fact the rule of strict equality between Muslims was scarcely applied after its promulgation, at least when one considers the privileges accorded in the primitive Muslim community to the Prophet's relatives or to his oldest disciples. Whatever difference there may have been after Muhammad's death over the person of his successor, some favouring 'Ali, his cousin and son-in-law, others Abū Bakr, his closest friend, it is true that in the early days the Companions, considered to be the oldest adherents of Islam, always held a pre-eminent position, enjoying notably much larger stipends than the other members of the community and occupying in the transmission of the Tradition a special position suited to nourishing their personal ambitions.

Indeed these privileges could have become still more important subsequently if the first Islamic community had followed 'Ali and adopted the principles which later characterised Shi'ism. We have in fact seen that according to these principles, the imāms, successors of the Prophet, were reputed to enjoy superhuman qualities, such as impeccability, and that their whole family, the family of the Prophet, was considered 'pure'. The society corresponding exactly to such a conception, which was barely realised except under the Fātimid caliphate (909–1171), could only be a strongly hierarchical society whose head, reputedly descended from Muhammad, and considered to be the sole interpreter of religious doctrine, occupied the summit, surrounded by his closest relatives; then we would find those initiated into the esoteric doctrine, who formed a sort of aristocracy not relying in any way on birth, since it included non-Arabs as well as Arabs, provided they had passed the necessary stages; then came the simple members of the Ismā'īlī movement, not initiated into the secrets because of their intellectual incapacity; and finally there followed the Muslims hostile to this doctrine, and, in the last place, the non-Muslims. The hierarchisation of the whole was based on religious values, or more precisely on the existence of a group of people empowered to guarantee the functioning of the state by reason of their adherence to doctrine which was its official doctrine. However, and despite the theoretical rigidity of this situation, there have in fact to be some qualifications: non-adhering Muslims preserved, for example, in the Fātimid environment, the right to teach, at least at certain periods; on the other hand, and following a constant tradition in the Islamic world, non-Muslims could be admitted as political counsellors and sometimes entrusted with the highest functions, of which that of vizier was one; finally the slave mercenaries who surrounded the ruler played, at least through their chiefs, a not insignificant role in politics, while economic activity was dominated by great merchants who belonged to different religions.

Such then was the type of organisation, the first place being reserved for the members of a politico-religious movement, which experienced in the Fātimid period an initial application corresponding to the originality of Shi'ite thought within Islam, but of which certain characteristics were equally recognisable in the first Sunnite Muslim community. The latter, while not recognising charismatic qualities in the leaders which it accepted or agreed to recognise, was always in fact, if not a hierarchical society based on a fundamental ideology and also taking account of birth, at least a non-egalitarian society some of whose members merited preferential treatment by reason of their family origins.

Thus in particular there was distinguished from the beginning the caste of Arab fighters, who had been the instruments of the astonishing Arab-Islamic conquest, and who received on this account pensions varying according to the 'merits' which they could show. The former Emigrants and their descendants, then the Medinan Helpers and their descendants, then those called the 'Followers', succeeded one another in this respect in an order of classification of the Companions of the Prophet; this at first played an important role, then became progressively weaker, but perpetuated itself, for example, through the idea that the order of succession of the first caliphs corresponded to the order of their respective merits.

In the 'Abbāsid period, and doubtless from the end of the Umayyad period, the primitive system whereby stipends were paid to the descendants of the first fighters was no longer in force. Instead the pre-eminence of another category of Muslims was always recognised, namely those who enjoyed the dignity attached to being members of the Prophet's family, that is to say, the dignity of Hāshimites. The latter included both the descendants of Fātima and 'Ali, or 'Alids, who were generally hostile to the established régime, and the descendants of the Prophet's uncle, al-'Abbās, to whom the reigning caliphs belonged.

At the beginning of the ninth century, 30,000 Hāshimites are said to have received a stipend, symbolic in fact, but which none the less affirmed their social rank, and they found themselves represented by a trustee (*naqīb*) charged with the oversight of their interests. At the end of the tenth century and under the domination of the 'great Būyid emirs' of Shi'ite sympathy, a beginning was made to divide them into two branches, that of the 'Alids and that of the 'Abbāsids, each having its own trustee. Both kept some privileges, even in the tenth century, for example that of providing preachers for the central mosque of the capital, and they continued afterwards to be the object of a respect which, from the fourteenth century approximately, no longer applied except to the 'Alids, the 'sharīfs'. The latter had acquired, for some time already, a predominant position in the holy cities of Arabia, where, from the tenth century onwards and thanks to support from the Fātimids of Egypt, they had set up a small hereditary state which was to maintain itself, despite various vicissitudes, until the present century. What is more, they continued to enjoy, until recent times, a prestige which found itself illustrated in particular in the history of the extreme Maghrib.

The non-egalitarian character of the first Sunnite society owed less to the privileges enjoyed by members of the Prophet's family than to the attitude adopted in favour of Arabs of birth throughout the early period, that is, at least until the appearance of the 'Abbāsid caliphate in 750. It has often been said that the Umayyad empire was an 'Arab empire'. It was in fact governed by Arab caliphs, descended from the Quraysh tribe of whom the Prophet was already part, surrounded by the chiefs of the great Arab families, who, if need be, combined to give the power to one of their number. The army was composed only of Arabs, at least in the East, and even in the West, the place of the Arabs remained preponderant compared with that of the Berber troops who, as we know, had been associated with the invasion of Spain.

Confronting the Arabs, who were charged with political or war-like responsibilities or were great merchants, for mercantile enterprises were for the most part in the hands of the former caravan organisers, was the immense mass of the conquered peoples, most of whom were tributaries, subject to taxes which underlined their different status. Prominent among the latter were the agriculturalists, but there were also administrators, specialists in matters of finance, who had continued to be used in the offices of the capital or the provinces, even when they had remained faithful to their original religion.

Then, quite soon, there appeared between these two categories, as we have seen above a propos of the forms of the conquests, a third group, that of the 'converts' called *mawālī*. These were distinguished from the tributaries, but even they were not treated on an equal footing with the Arabs: they had no access to military functions, had generally to keep their former activities as producers of resources for the empire, in particular as artisans and cultivators, and then had above all to remain on the lands where, despite the efforts of certain caliphs like the celebrated 'Umar II, they did not enjoy the fiscal privileges accorded to the Arab occupiers who had become proprietors of former estates. As administrators, these converts were on the other hand able to attain to important functions, since they alone were able to calculate the sum total of the taxes and to keep registers, which, until the end of the seventh century, continued to be drawn up in the local languages, Pahlavi, Greek or Latin as the case might be, and which for a long time had Greek, not Arabic, numerals. They themselves had besides been initiated at the same time into the use of the Arabic language which certain of them adopted to draw up treatises on the art of governing or of counselling a ruler, introducing into the Islamic world a whole tradition on the methods of government borrowed from previous experiences.

But despite the rank to which some of these converted natives had gradually attained, a rank which was often due to their personal ability rather than to their functions, it is very certain that at the end of the first century of the Hijra, the Arabs continued, as in the beginning, to hold what we call the 'levers of control': the society of that era was thus a closely compartmentalised society, setting up a division between Muslims and non-Muslims and within the category of Muslims, between Arabs and non-Arabs. In one sense this latter division was even more clear than the first, in so far as it was impossible for a non-Arab to become or to pass himself off as an Arab; on the contrary, a movement of conversion, which was irreversible, had the effect of causing the number of non-Muslims to diminish progressively in favour of the Muslims. Thus it came about that the new converts, more and more numerous and always kept in an inferior position, clamoured for an adjustment. This was one of the factors of the revolution which, in the middle of the eighth century, corresponded to a transformation of the primitive Islamic society which became the complex and fluid ''Abbāsid' society after bringing to power the new dynasty of this name.

2 Social transformations in the 'Abbāsid period (750–1260)

In the early 'Abbāsid period, that is, between 750 and 945, there were important transformations taking place in the social structure. Whatever may have been the exact causes of the change of régime, causes which will doubtless always continue to be discussed, it is clear that the revolt took shape and grew, thanks to the support of the Iranian *mawāli*, especially the Khorasanians. Certainly the latter did not constitute solely and by themselves, as has sometimes tended to be said, an army which made room for a certain number of Arab chiefs; but the propaganda of the 'Abbāsid partisans was first addressed to them as elements of the population dissatisfied with their lot and only affected secondarily the Arab elements who also wished some change and a better assimilation of the non-Arabs.

After the victory, at any rate, the triumphant army, the support of the régime, retained within its ranks a part of the soldiery. The movement towards assimilation thus initiated, restricted at first to followers of the new caliph, soon extended to all the Iranian or Iraqi 'clients', who were officially admitted to military duties and were even preferred to the Arabs whom the 'Abbāsids distrusted. At the same time these people occupied an ever greater place in the service of the rulers, as the celebrated text of the Iranian Ibn al-Muqaffa' shows, who, despite his origins, disapproved of this policy; he saw in it an inopportune 'democratisation' of the caliphal court, and on the contrary recommended to the representatives of a Hāshimite dynasty not to deprive themselves of the support of members of their family. In fact the protestations of an Ibn al-Muqaffa' were in vain; the *mawāli* continued to work their way up even higher into the state machinery, and so it was that under Hārūn al-Rashīd the vizierate, an office which was only then beginning to appear, was held by the famous Yahyā the Barmakid, a man originally from Balkh in Khorasan whose ancestors were Buddhists. We have already seen that the action of the viziers varied according to the personality of the caliphs they served, but the progressive development, which their office experienced, corresponded to a precise sociological fact and to the increasing importance in the government and administration of the empire of the non-Arab 'secretaries'.

For this reason the first 'supporters' of the movement who were often called 'sons of the régime', and on whom the 'Abbāsid rulers had at first conferred honours and responsibilities, were rapidly relegated to second place, and had no possibility of forming themselves into a new privileged class. An analogous phenomenon arose a little later, at the beginning of the ninth century, for other 'supporters'. At this moment the second son of the deceased caliph Hārūn al-Rashīd was at war with his brother and succeeded in taking from him both the caliphate and the central regions of the empire, thanks to the support of the Khorasanians who formed his 'party'. Ascending the throne under the name of al-Ma'mūn, the new ruler conferred on those who had helped him high positions in the army as well as in the provinces where he sent them as governors, and he also allowed them to work their way into the central administration. Anecdotes circulated about the incompetence, indeed the stupidity, of these men who, under the pretext that they had worked efficiently for al-Ma'mūn, aspired to any office, and we can understand how, once again, there was a move towards the formation of a society in which a superior place was reserved for a small category of men bound to the régime. But as in the first case, the favours thus dispensed were only temporary.

The society which emerged in the 'Abbāsid period and which was marked by no real ideological hierarchisation thus became a relatively egalitarian society as far as Muslims were concerned. We must stress the term 'relatively', however, because distinctions remained for the *mawāli* in particular; they had indeed been able to gain the right of playing an active and sometimes political role, but they remained *mawāli*, who had to content themselves in certain circumstances with an inferior place; at the time of al-Ma'mūn, for example, palace etiquette still imposed separate places for Arabs and non-Arabs and they were forbidden to mingle during the ceremonies. Even if afterwards we no longer find any trace of facts of this kind, some individuals are accused, in the biographical notices given over to them, of having forged false Arab genealogies, and this would seem to indicate that some prestige still attached to Arab birth.

The fact remains that a tendency towards the lessening of inequalities made itself felt more and more in the course of the two centuries marked by the effective government of the 'Abbāsid caliphs (from 750 to 945 approximately). This tendency prevailed all the more easily because the society included a number of slaves, men and women, who were very often set free. The concubines of this category, whose status changed when they became the mothers of a male child, were thus numerous in the harems of the caliphs, and their sons had no ban imposed on them, contrary to what had happened in the preceding era: not only were they able to reign just like the sons of free Arab mothers, but mostly it was they who for various reasons were chosen to ascend the throne. During these two centuries the caliphs were thus few who could boast a purely Arab origin, while at other levels also of society, the sons of Iranian, Greek, Turkish or black slave mothers, who were acknowledged as free because of their fathers and were treated on an equal footing with the pure Arabs, became more and more numerous, and while the former freed slaves, also more and more numerous, rejoined the great mass of 'clients'. A progressive disappearance of privileges followed for the Arab elements who were gradually swamped by the non-Arabs or by the children of mixed marriages.

The Arabs too, who had continued to fill partly the ranks of the army at the beginning of the 'Abbāsid period, even though the caliphs only had limited confidence in them, were, at the beginning of the ninth century, completely eliminated. After the civil war just mentioned, which for many years brought into conflict the two brothers al-Amīn and al-Ma'mūn, the idea took shape that it was better to use mercenaries of foreign origin, not involved directly with the internal affairs of the empire. The successor of al-Ma'mūn, al-Mu'tasim, therefore recruited a large number of Turkish slaves, whom he made the solid base of his troops, but whom he tried to keep well away from the population, especially by making it compulsory for them to marry wives of the same origin. Thus he created a sort of military class, whose role, according to him, was to protect the caliph and the régime without taking part in the palace struggles or in the political or religious internal quarrels. But the reverse happened, and the interference of this class in the conduct of the state took on proportions which became more and more disastrous as the officers of the guard, divided into rival clans, and often supporting different claimants, showed more boldness in saving their own interests, and did not hesitate in so doing to trigger off palace revolutions.

Thus al-Mutawakkil was assassinated in 861 following on a plot hatched by Turkish officers. Thus, too, during the period immediately following his death, the caliphs succeeded each other in rapid succession, 'made and unmade' by these same individuals. The old military caste of Arab aristocrats, with whom the Khorasanian mercenaries had mixed after the 'Abbāsid revolution, gave way from now on to a corps of Turkish mercenaries, of slave origin and recent conversion, but imbued with warrior-like strength and curiously impervious to the egalitarian ideal of the Islamic community. A new system of privileges was superimposed on the requirements of the religious Law, and the habits thus formed continued until the Turkish officers of Samarra were succeeded by the Daylamite emirs, that is to say, Iranians who belonged to the Būyid family and who seized power effectively from 945. It was the same when these emirs were in their turn ousted by the 'sultans' who appeared in the following century, and who established in all the countries of the Orient, in the Arab and Iranian regions as well as in the Anatolian countries, the yoke of a domination more foreign than ever to the local populations.

A fundamental characteristic of medieval Islamic society would thus have been, after as well as before the 'Abbāsid 'revolution', not to be able to do without a powerful military 'order', since this was necessary both for maintaining the established régime and also for the protection of the frontiers. This characteristic showed itself in the early days by the predominance of Arabs, who had the two-fold merit of being armed defenders of Islam and of belonging to the chosen race. Afterwards other ethnic groups worked themselves into the same role according to circumstances which varied from one region to another. We mentioned the case of the Turkish mercenaries at Samarra and of the Būyid princes. Again from the same period, for example in eastern Iran, certain autonomous governors, particularly from Transoxiana, had taken into their service Turkish tribes coming from the Asiatic steppes; these foreign troops later became emancipated and were able to found their own states and principalities, which were, however, integrated into the empire to the extent that their chiefs recognised the authority of the 'Abbāsid caliph and requested from him a formal investiture. Such was the experience of the Ghaznavids who became masters of what is now Afghanistan, undertook the conquest of India, and, like the Iranian Būyids, attained a remarkable degree of power. Such was also, in a certain way, the experience of the Seljuks who streamed into Iran at the head of their Turcoman armies, threw themselves into impressive territorial conquests, and imposed themselves in their turn on the 'Abbāsid caliph. Their ascendancy, however, took place in a new climate because these Turkish chiefs of recent conversion, who, like their predecessors, took up the defence of Islam, and who obtained from the caliph a title of 'sultan' destined to be a lasting favour, brought with them tribal groups anxious to become established in a Muslim country and numerous enough to change the balance of society.

The results obtained under their impetus were moreover different in each case. In a non-Muslim country like Anatolia, which was conquered by them for Islam, the Turks, newly arrived, behaved almost like the Arabs at the time of the first conquests; in other long islamised regions, on the contrary, they were content to identify with the ruling military caste. But they in their turn soon found themselves in the situation of using the services of other ethnic groups such as the Kurds, who entered their armies in the Zengid era and who themselves later founded a dynasty, that of the Ayyūbids, with multiple ramifications. These are so many typical examples taken from the history of the Islamic East, to which could be added others, taken mainly from the history of the West, which would contribute further to demonstrate the same fact: how often Islamic society, during the centuries which preceded the Mongol invasion of 1260, experienced successive changes due to a continual supply of new ethnic elements in the form of more or less organised armed bands.

Indeed these new elements did not care about Islam as such; but their coming was without doubt facilitated, if not provoked, by the conditions in which Islam had spread. On the one hand, the great empire, whose birth had been brought about by the expansion of Islam, could not maintain itself without the action of a strong army, recruited by preference from among the foreigners who protected its territory after having infiltrated it; on the other hand, such an empire was not defended in such a way that the thrust of invaders on one or other of its frontiers could have been held. It is, however, remarkable that such invaders have never, at least in the medieval period which interests us, tried to escape from the framework created by Islamic civilisation and that on the contrary they have adopted it to ensure their own authority, thus testifying to the prestige retained by the Commander of the Faithful even when his own troops had failed to maintain the security at the centre of the *dār al-Islām*.

As the effect of a political situation more and more troubled, the ethnic mosaic formed by the populations of the 'Abbāsid empire thus only became more complicated with time, while Islam continued to proclaim egalitarian principles between peoples of different origins which only gradually took effect. Moreover the new elements introduced by the sale of slave mercenaries, or brought in with the stream of invasions, consisted essentially of soldiers. The intermingling of races, which had operated at the beginning of the 'Abbāsid period, could no longer occur in these conditions, nor permit the assimilation of these soldiers of varying origin, who did not cease to pour in, and whose officers attained to the highest posts, while at the same time receiving land concessions assuring their independence and allowing them to maintain the troops they commanded. This implied the appearance of a novel social group ready to assert itself against the Arab and arabised populations of the empire.

3 Ethnic groups and social environments

The racial heterogeneity of the Muslim population during the ʻAbbāsid period had not in fact been without influence on the various strata which then composed ʻAbbāsid society. The army, whose pre-eminence in political life did not cease to make itself felt, had in this regard, as we have just seen, a well-marked character. At first composed of Arabs established in Syria, it had later welcomed Khorasanians who were chiefly Iranians. Later these Iranians gave way to Turks, who were joined later by the Iranian Daylamites and later still by the Kurds, while in the west the Berbers entered the Muslim armies in larger numbers, and while everywhere the palace guards were formed of slaves who might be black in Egypt, European in Spain. In each case the companies of different ethnic membership were strictly separated, and could be assigned distinct missions, thus avoiding all confusion.

In the administrative offices and services, on the other hand, the Iranians, converts or not, were dominant, being outstanding for their knowledge of secretarial work and methods. It is true that administrators of different origin were to be found in Syria, Egypt, and in all the countries conquered by the Arabs; but they never possessed the same ability to make a career in important posts. The Iranians in fact combined technical competence with a long familiarity with the rules of *savoirvivre*, thanks to manuals of good conduct which their traditional literature produced for those close to kings and the great. Thus they understood the art of serving the rulers, and of guiding and helping them in governmental tasks, something which could only gradually be assimilated by the Arab authors who were soon writing epistles on the same subject.

These same Iranians had been favoured by the first 'Abbāsid caliphs, who owed them their coming to power, and who chose from among them their colleagues and secretaries. Subsequently, and through regional solidarity, the Iranian *kuttāb* in office preferred to recruit, as their assistants, fellow countrymen whose specialisation in this activity did not cease to grow. This was so much the case that the Seljuk sultans, when they took power in the eleventh century, in their turn had recourse to Iranian administrators, of whom the most celebrated representative was the minister Nizām al-Mulk.

Without doubt the situation was a little different in the Fātimid state, which combined with its Shi'ite orientation the fact of having taken shape in the Berber country of Ifriqiyya, and then in Egypt. However, there too the administrators belonged, by reason of a recruitment whose forms varied, to a partly native society where on several occasions 'tributaries', Jews or Christians, were seen to figure. Only the régimes which followed each other in Muslim Spain seem to have succeeded in giving such tasks to native Arabs, and so to have created a different type of secretarial class; this case, however, was that of an outlying province of restricted size, whose problems only rarely matched those which presented themselves in the rest of the empire.

Everywhere moreover in fact the administrators formed, if not a group apart, at least a closed community, consisting mainly of Iranians, who might be joined by Mesopotamians, and above all characterised by a culture quite different from that boasted by the other elements of society. Not only had the members of this 'caste' in general a technical training enabling them to deal without difficulty with fiscal problems, which in themselves had not changed with the appearance of Islam. But they were also more often permeated with Iranian maxims and legends, for which they retained an unbounded admiration, and which they rediscovered in the Arab translations of the *Book of Kalila and Dimna* or in various didactic writings once in vogue at the court of the Sassanids, dealing with court etiquette and everyday manners. From all these texts there emanated a wisdom and a morality which, without being opposed to Islamic teaching, were distinct from it to the extent that they were drawn from their own sources, being based simultaneously on the beliefs of the Iranian, Zoroastrian or Manichean religions and on the philosophical doctrines of late antiquity which had penetrated the circles of the Sassanid era.

Thus the administrators or *kuttāb* at the beginning of the 'Abbāsid era found themselves launching the so-called Shu'ūbite movement, of which we have already seen some implications, but whose cultural aspect had for its object to emphasise the value of the Iranian heritage while limiting the sway of Koranic revelation. They were not in the end successful, and the ultimate balance rested simultaneously on the working of Islamic principles and on the ancient traditions which they defended. But they continued no less to show their particular interest in the non-religious sciences derived from classical thought, especially philosophy, which at this period embraced them all. Thus they numbered in their group, at the time of the Būyid emirs, fervent disciples of Mu'tazilite rationalism, practised in particular by certain viziers. Later, with the arrival of the Turkish Seljuks, they continued to form a group quite distinct from that of the military aristocracy but displayed opinions on the whole more in conformity with traditional doctrine. Thus they moved closer to the men of religion whose support they sought against the Turkish sultans whose power seemed to them sometimes disturbing.

It is true that this class of administrator did not remain totally isolated and turned in on itself. We know of the cases of several individuals who succeeded in insinuating themselves into it, even though they did not possess initially the necessary training or had not been born in this milieu. Such a one was the vizier of the caliph al-Mu'tasim, a certain Ibn al-Zayyāt, a merchant's son as his name indicates, who, while still very young, was outstanding for his intellectual abilities; such, too, was at the same period, al-Fadl ibn Marwān, a landowner honoured by the king; and again, a little later, there was Yahyā ibn Khākān, a man of Turkish origin who managed to become the intimate of the caliph al-Mutawakkil. The possibility that the sovereign might choose, if he wished, some obscure individual to make him his friend and later confide to him important duties, opened to all an administrative career, to all those at least who had succeeded in gaining access to the court, which was not always easy, and who had proved themselves to have a subtle and ambitious spirit. However, it seems that at the end of the ninth century the class of secretary showed itself to be more often closed than formerly, the tasks having become more technical and the chance person having no longer the possibility of rising to the vizierate: the vizier was then normally a financial specialist, who had to have held previously important positions in central or provincial administration.

Thus despite events which brought about changes in the social structures between the seventh and the thirteenth centuries, military men and administrators continued during this period to exist as distinct social groups, opposed even ethnically. It is to be noted, however, that on this last point the rule was not absolute, for the Iranians who dominated the secretarial circles very soon became equally part of the army. It might even be asked if certain supposed Turks of Samarra were not rather Iranian, like the Daylamites of the Būyid period, and it is known that inversely Turks by origin had their place among the courtiers and administrators.

Alongside the military and administrative personnel, the men of religion formed at any rate the third important group of 'Abbāsid Islamic society, a group very much apart from the two others, but also more varied in its representatives and their origins. Arabs and non-Arabs mingled indeed in such a way that it is impossible to establish, even to sketch out, a semblance of statistics concerning the racial or regional origins of its members. From another angle, there can be discerned among them various internal categories, comprising both the 'theorists' such as jurists and theologians, and the 'practitioners' like the cadis, and the training and the role of the two could only be fused with difficulty.

Of the cadis, it will be recalled, no very deep legal knowledge was demanded; they simply had to know how to apply the legal regulations familiar to every good Muslim, and to pass sentences based on equity. Assisted by professional jurists who gave a ruling on certain cases by giving consultations, they could also have recourse to other specialists in dealing with delicate problems of inheritance.

Among the theorists, on the contrary, the *fuqahā'* or jurisconsults had to know all the details of legal prescriptions touching social life and liturgical activities, while the traditionists devoted their activity to collecting prophetic Traditions, the source of essential teachings concerning law or doctrine. As for the theologians, they remained rather on the periphery – to the extent that theology developed late and that the recognition of its usefulness was always a subject for discussion. The theologians did not train disciples in a regular way, since in the eleventh century theology or *kalām* was not even included among the sciences taught in the madrasas, and since Tradition or the strictly Koranic sciences were pursued in establishments specially reserved for that purpose. However it seems that the theologians may have had their place in certain colleges by the expedient of preaching (*wa'z*) which was provided for in a school like the Nizāmiyya, the first school in Baghdad, and which involved the spread of theological doctrines. In this era, moreover, the 'preachers' of this kind – to distinguish them from those who pronounced the official sermon at the Friday Prayer – could come and go as they liked at court, where they were received alongside the *fuqahā'* and the *kuttāb*. They were apparently given the task of defending sound doctrine, which was not however exactly the same, depending on whether they obeyed the policy of the caliph or that of the sultans and their viziers.

The various individuals we have just enumerated deserved anyway to be also grouped together under the title of '*ulamā*', the 'scholars or doctors', alongside whom the ascetics (*zuhhād*) also sometimes featured, whose most eminent representatives were admitted into the caliph's circle. All had in common a concern for the dignity which went with their position, and which obliterated the original differences between Arabs of birth and arabised non-Arabs when they had acquired the same degree of science or authority. In fact we know the Arab descent of celebrated founders of legal schools like Mālik, Ibn Hanbal and al-Shāfi'i, whereas Abū Hanīfa was descended from a freedman; we also know the Arab descent of the leading traditionists of the Umayyad period, al-Awzā'i and al-Zuhri. But the authors of the six great 'canonical' collections of traditions which appeared in the 'Abbāsid era were in large part descended from families of former tributaries; such were al-Bukhāri, al-Tirmidhi and al-Nasā'i, whose names even suggest Iranian descent, not to mention Muslim, whose surname al-Nīsābūri is equally significant, and Ibn Māja, a native of Qazwin, whereas doubt remains about Dāwūd called al-Sijistāni, which is Iranian, since he is also al-Azdi, which indicates that he belonged or was attached to the tribe of Azd. If we know, however, the importance of the role played by the veritable dynasties of cadis of Arab origin, like that of the Banū Abī l-Shawārib, who enjoyed a certain prestige in Iraq in the tenth century, we find on the part of the theologians a slightly different situation: among these, Arabs by birth like Ibn Hanbal or al-Ash'ari, defended traditional ideas; but the rationalising doctrines were generally developed by non-Arabs, such as the Mesopotamian or Iranian *mawāli* known as the first Mu'tazilites. Again, many Ash'arite theologians of moderate views were Iranians, like al-Juwayni or the great al-Ghazāli, both natives of eastern Iran. The founder too, or aspiring founder, of the Māturīdite theological school, al-Māturīdi, was descended from a family from Transoxiana. Similarly again, the spread of the Ash'arite school was assured above all by the individuals who at first taught in Mesopotamia or Iran and later found themselves called to Syria to teach in the newly founded madrasas there. Finally Iranians were equally present in Syria among the Hanbalites, since one of the chief families that was part of this community at Damascus in the thirteenth century was originally from Shiraz, while another was of Arab origin, and a third came from Palestine without its ethnic origin being definitely known.

Thus we observe that the 'doctors' of Iranian origin did not cease to play leading roles in this society, while enjoying the freedom to spread somewhat advanced ideas there. In

Sūfi circles, where sometimes divergent movements appeared, it was the same, and Iranians in particular there propagated a tendency that might be called heterodox, that of the mystics professing a monism contrary to divine transcendence, who were sometimes the object of severe condemnation and who were perhaps subjected to the influence of older religious doctrines more or less impregnated with gnosticism. The same observation holds for the orientation of the philosophers who remained on the periphery of orthodoxy; among these some Arabs certainly became renowned, such as the famous al-Kindi and Ibn Tufayl, but they were dominated above all by non-Arabs like al-Fārābi, Ibn Sīnā and Miskawayh in the east, doubtless also Ibn Rushd in the west.

The social group of the men of religion and the intellectuals in the broad sense, where individuals of a very varied ethnic origin contributed to a common development of the sciences, thus reflected fairly faithfully in its composition the heterogeneity which had characterised Arab-Islamic society from the beginning of the 'Abbāsid period and which had afterwards continued to become more marked. The very reduced place held by the Arab element among the doctors in the thirteenth century, for example, corresponded to that which they had come to occupy in a society in continual growth, in which foreigners had not ceased to merge by adopting the Muslim faith and way of thinking, which they also helped to modify. But, as a social group representing a whole society, this group of men of religion none the less kept its individuality while in no way resembling a closed caste.

It did not in fact enjoy any definite status nor any privilege of whatever kind, and remained open to whoever possessed the qualities of knowledge, intelligence or piety needed to belong to it. Hence the fluidity of its boundary, and the absence of uniformity in the habits and modes of life of the people who formed it, and who in fact came under different categories. Some among them belonged to great families of cadis, jurists and traditionists; but there were also many among them whose social level and fortune are little known to us, if not completely unknown. The resources which both had at their disposal for living only rarely matched their quality as doctors and we must assume that most of those who did not occupy an official paid position either enjoyed a personal income or practised parallel activities connected with commerce or manufacture. Hence the non-existence, as it were, from an economic point of view, of a social class whose members, on this level, did not enjoy independence.

The situation was only modified in the eleventh century when the sultans and the dignitaries in their entourage founded colleges or madrasas, establishments provided with their own revenues, allowing them to pay the professors of law, the preachers and the readers of the Koran. In this era a body of '*ulamā*' was formed, mentioned in particular by al-Ghazāli in his works. Its members, who from then on played a more precise role in public affairs and who were often supported by governments, sometimes showed their disapproval of the general policy, thus obliging the rulers to modify their line of action. At the same time the new system of teaching, which spread across the Islamic world from east to west, facilitated the rise of less fortunate young men, coming sometimes from rural communities, and this widened the recruitment of scholars and made them subject henceforth to the power which had arranged their training.

Previously the doctors sought more and more to keep their distance *vis-à-vis* the governors, and it was very exceptional for a caliph like al-Mutawakkil to have had recourse to traditionists in order to refute the Mu'tazilite theses, after al-Ma'mūn had personally favoured the holders of the rationalising doctrine. But the men of law and of thought, gladly listened to by the great, and enjoying the respect of the lower classes, had no less shown themselves already to be the natural intermediaries between the ruler or the prince and the great mass of the people; this constituted the throng of 'subjects' with activities profitable for the state, whose fundamental character of Muslims hardly obliterated the differences existing between merchants and artisans, on the one hand, and agriculturalists, on the other hand, who were condemned by their isolation to a still lower position.

We know that the artisans from the towns, grouped in guilds, were often shopkeepers at the same time. Manufacturers of small objects also saw to their retail sale, and the merchants of a given product were installed near each other in the same place, following an ancient principle which was always applied but which does not concern us here. What must be here underlined is the fact that these artisans and merchants were not part, at the height of the Middle Ages, of any autonomous professional organisation. Admittedly the problem of corporations in the Islamic countries has often been discussed, and it has for long been thought that the groupings of this kind, which still existed at the dawn of the contemporary world, went back to a distant past; hypotheses have even been formulated about the links which might have existed between such groupings and the Ismā'īli movement, which was particularly favourable to manual workers. But further research has shown that there was in reality no trace in an earlier period of corporate organisations such as these. We know of guilds then, which each had a kind of agent to represent it, generally called *'arīf*, but the craftsmen remained no less under the direct control of the authorities and in particular of the *muhtasib*. Thus the members of a profession never seem to have enjoyed any advantage, and still less the right to admit a newcomer into their midst by an initiation ceremony.

Quite distinct from the small traders and artisans were the merchants who arranged the transfer of merchandise from town to town or from country to country and who benefited from quite a different consideration. Some of them were content to finance, thanks to their own private means, various enterprises, but without being personally involved in them. To do their business most of them moved along the caravan roads or the busy maritime routes of the Mediterranean and the Indian Ocean. All of them, too, possessed lands, which thus formed an indispensable and solid source of capital, although particularly vulnerable in the case of confiscation.

These business men who could serve equally as money changers and sometimes as bankers, were counted among the 'notables' (*a'yān*) of their place of residence. Their situation varied however from one city to another, and at Baghdad, for example, they had to be satisfied with carrying on business at a distance from the court to which only the richest among them penetrated. There too, moreover, a change made itself felt when authority passed into the hands of professional soldiers, more often than not foreigners; in contrast to these, the members of a layer of population longer arabised, came to represent the ancient Arabo-Islamic tradition. Thus the opposition between the great businessmen, often of Arab descent, and the shopkeepers from the local petit bourgeoisie was progressively obliterated.

For their part, the cultivators remained most often isolated from the inhabitants of the towns and experienced very varied status. Some of them were masters and owners of their land; this was frequently the case in Iran where the former landed proprietors had remained where they were at the conquest; it was more rarely the case in Mesopotamia where many of the lands conquered by force had been handed over to court dignitaries, and also in Syria where the surrender of regions by treaty had not hindered many of the small farmers fleeing for good into Byzantine territory. There were also, and in particular among them, many tenant farmers who had more or less advantageous contracts and were employed on the great estates, whose revenues went at first to the Arab leaders, then to the favourites of the caliphs, then, from the middle of the tenth century, to military leaders. These cultivators were, except in Arabia, nearly all natives and non-Arabs while the proprietors, on whom they depended and who enjoyed this advantage by virtue of theoretically temporary 'concessions', had most often arrived late, did not reside on their lands and thus were unlike feudal 'lords', all the more so because they remained without any power of jurisdiction. An intermediate group, however, was formed by the small proprietors of Iran who had kept their own lands after the conquest.

As to the non-Muslims, it may be noted that they did not form a social group apart, even when they belonged to communities which had their own rules in things concerning family matters. Indeed they found themselves integrated into some of the groups that we have just described. If they were not able to attain to military posts, nor apparently to be made part of the group of Muslim doctors, they were able to practise the role of administrator and thus to attain to high positions. Most of them were cultivators, artisans or merchants, and some occupations, like that of moneychanger (for the Jews) or physician (for the Christians), were more specially adopted by them though not reserved for them. Thus they participated in all the activities of the productive sectors.

4 Hierarchy and social tensions

Imperfectly bound up with the ethnic groups with which some of them were confused, the principal social groups which have just been enumerated do not present as such any cohesion or stability, while their reciprocal relationships varied from time to time and from region to region. The situation was not the same in the 'Abbāsid East, where the Iranian 'secretaries' played an important role and from a sociological point of view formed a very special group of secular humanists and literati, and in the West, where administrative posts were often handed down to Arabs by birth, and where, on the other hand, the members of the magistrature had access to governmental responsibilities. It was different again in the so-called Seljuk East, where a rapprochement came about between secretaries and '*ulamā*', and where the magistrates sometimes became political counsellors of the ruler. But there was always a sharp separation made between the groups thus distinguished by the nature of their dominant activities, even if these groups did not constitute castes or even, properly speaking, 'classes'. Indeed it would be difficult to know whether to use the term 'class' for these social groups, which themselves possessed internally their own hierarchy; this was transcended in fact by another distinction, extremely common among Arab authors, that which placed the aristocracy (*al-khāssa*) over against the people (*al-'āmma*). This aristocracy was, according to some observations, made up essentially of individuals belonging to different groups, and living around or near the ruler or prince. But nothing is more difficult than to define it precisely, even at a given period; we can only to some extent discern the leading persons of the four groups we have just distinguished. In the military group it was the superior offices, that is, the emirs, with important responsibilities in the directing of warlike expeditions or the maintenance of internal order, who belonged to it; they were the supports of the régime and figured among the dignitaries who were present at general audiences and who sometimes served as counsellors to the sovereign. Similarly among the administrators, the leading civil servants of the capital represented in some way the body of secretaries, and were also numbered among the dignitaries. Among the magistrates, the cadis of the capital held an outstanding position, since on them depended the fate of numerous individuals called before the high courts presided over by the caliph, notably at the beginning of the tenth century in Baghdad. Certain scholars and certain ascetics were also admitted to audiences, especially to those where the caliph made proclamations of a doctrinal nature which he wanted to see spread in the provinces. The men of religion were therefore present to give their backing to the caliph's policy, and at the same time to guarantee the carrying out of the instructions given. As for the great merchants, though they did not belong officially to the ruler's entourage, by exercising their function of bankers as well as of merchants, they could furnish the ruler with funds when the latter had treasury difficulties, and as a result of this might find themselves in direct relationship with him; thus the 'Abbāsid caliph al-Muqtadir, at the beginning of the tenth century, had recourse to the services of Jewish merchants known as the 'court bankers'. Modelled on the aristocracy thus gravitating round the caliph, there was similarly in the provinces an aristocracy, perhaps inferior, round each governor or each local dynast. In no case was it an aristocracy of birth, but only a collection of men, influential for different reasons, who because of this, were indispensable to the ruler or his representative in helping him to carry out efficiently his governmental tasks. The autocratic character of all the systems of government found in medieval Islam created this aristocracy of a particular type, whose members belonged, again in very uneven fashion, to the principal social groups we have distinguished. The military leaders, except in rare moments, had however a much more important place among them than most of the other dignitaries, and the 'productive' sector was on the whole sacrificed, whether it was the merchants, normally strangers at the court, or the agriculturalists, totally unrecognised, at least unless they were confused with the owners of great estates.

The type of society thus established, although described in this perhaps over-simplified way, long remained typical of Islamic civilisation, though it cannot be said to be truly inspired by the principles of Islam; rather it was the result of the political order set up in Islamic countries. The two values which there conferred superior rank were in fact the service of the ruler on the one hand, and the service of religion on the other hand – in certain circumstances the two might be confused – without account being taken of a capacity for economic output which would ensure the equilibrium of this same society. We would be therefore right in speaking of a society of 'orders', but with changing boundaries and extremely variable relative influence.

We know, for example, that the men of religion had from the tenth century a right of audience with the caliph or sultan, which they did not have previously. In the same way the merchants in the tenth century obtained both a consideration and a political power, which later they no longer had because of the decline of big business in Baghdad. In the same way, again, the seizure of power by sultans of Turkish origin, accompanied by an army almost exclusively Turkish, created a new rift in society, and brought about a rapprochement between the administrators and the men of religion who, a little later in the fourteenth century, became the 'men of the turban' over against the men of the sword.

This society of orders, imperfectly defined in their relationship with one another, also saw produced frequently, in different circumstances, more or less violent reactions, showing that all these elements were not perfectly integrated into a whole. There was at first the case of the slaves, who had become very numerous in 'Abbāsid society – whether they were bought in Central Asia or East Africa or had been captured on expeditions into infidel country – and who had all sorts of occupations. Many were employed as domestics in families, and experienced a lot of which they did not complain; some were soon freed, especially concubine wives if they gave birth to a son. Other slaves served in the army, where sometimes brilliant careers were open to them. But many too were employed as agricultural workers on large estates. Such was the case of the Zanj, black slaves who were given the task of cultivating the old swamps of lower Iraq. The Zanj rebelled at the end of the ninth century and by their determination forced the caliphate to undertake costly and difficult military expeditions; their movement corresponds in fact to all those which were stirred up by the peasant fieldworkers, whose condition was particularly harsh; these occured in various regions, including Iran at the beginning of the 'Abbāsid period, Egypt on various occasions, and Syria in the ninth century.

But beside the agricultural labourers, whether slaves or not, there were other recalcitrant elements. There existed in the large towns a proletariat made up of underprivileged persons and of small artisans, who united and who willingly demonstrated when there were civil wars or troubles of various origin, such as those experienced in Iraq between the ninth and the eleventh centuries. It was this proletariat which fought alongside the troops of the caliph al-Amīn in the famous siege of Baghdad, thus taking sides against the pretensions of al-Ma'mūn and perhaps against his bold religious policy; it was they who, later on various occasions, staged violent demonstrations directed against the wealthy. These 'brigands' (*'ayyārūn*), as they were called, had none the less an ideal of generosity, which cemented their associations, and they willingly took up their stance on the periphery of the established order, while also taking part in the religious wars frequent in Iraq at this period. Elsewhere there came together, especially in the towns of Iraq, groups of 'youths' (*fityān*) who re-established peace where the central authority had lost all influence. Elsewhere, too, groups of artisans took over local power and this phenomenon produced a dynasty like that of the Saffārids of Sistan. Further west, in Syria, similar demonstrations are recorded, due this time to other associations of 'youths' (*ahdāth*) directed by a leader (*ra'īs*) who sometimes fought the established régime (for example, that of the Fātimids in the eleventh century), sometimes co-operated with it, right up to the moment when the Seljuk Turks used a police force directly dependent on the official power. Indeed, and despite recent researches, it remains difficult to define the exact origin of the different groups whose activities are thus mentioned in the early histories, and to determine whether or not they obeyed what is sometimes called an 'ideology'. But the study of the best-known facts, those of Syria, shows that the source of the demonstrations cannot be reduced to a single phenomenon.

Parallel with this, above all from the beginning of the twelfth century, we know of treatises about *futuwwa*, a term belonging to the same root as *fatā*, pl. *fityān*, 'youth'. Such works expound the community ideal of some of these groups, although we cannot establish a precise link between the information of the historians and these theoretical considerations. Always it seems that the members of this *futuwwa*, doubtless a little different from that of the 'brigands' of the ninth and tenth centuries, practised an initiation rite which recalled that of the mystic brotherhoods, while they legitimised their working gains by preaching a pooling of the surplus. Such an ideology, of whose precise hold little is known in the classical period, seems to have spread mostly in the artisan group, and to have been in some sort of competition at the end of the twelfth century, with the Sūfi movement. This would explain why the caliph al-Nāsir, at the turn of the twelfth and thirteenth centuries, tried to rely on them in order to make this ideology that of the entire Islamic community united under his authority. Al-Nāsir's undertaking, if it had succeeded, might perhaps have created a new social hierarchy based on membership of the *futuwwa*.

But, to return to the causes of social troubles, we must also take into account the fact that, in the Syrian towns of the tenth and eleventh centuries, the discontented were not always the underprivileged or the labourers. The notables too and the representatives of big business could have seen their interests threatened by the policy of the rulers of the time, for example, by the policy which led to the concluding of a commercial treaty in 969 between the Hamdānid emir and the Byzantines. It even came about that these merchants sought their independence when official power no longer seemed to secure their effective protection, thus it was that at the end of the eleventh century, on the eve of the Crusades, the two towns of Tyre and Tripoli, which had become rich under the Fātimid regime, threw off its yoke and set up principalities governed by cadis coming from the merchant class. Over against the revolts of the poor, we must place those of the rich, and into this last category might even fall the palace revolutions, generally due to officers of the caliph's bodyguard, who enjoyed the support of certain dignitaries. There again the revolutions were generally linked with struggles for influence, in which various motives could play a part, religious as well as political.

Finally it would not do to forget the role, more often than not disruptive, played by the nomads, whatever their origin (Arabs, Turks, Berbers), who sometimes undertook to insinuate themselves into urban society, indeed even to dominate it, and sometimes were content with wreaking havoc, and then deliberately remained among the non-integrated elements. Thus it frequently happened that very varied circumstances might cause social tensions or revolts, and that various elements considering themselves 'oppressed' might react against the established order.

Islamic society none the less kept a hierarchical and compartmentalised form, which in part rested on an aristocratic organisation of power, and whose origin was both religious and secular, due in part to historic circumstances which were present at the setting-up of the Arab Islamic empire. Alongside religious doctrine the tradition of 'oriental despotism' weighed heavily in fact on the evolution of the countries of Islam, and the diversity of ethnic groups, whose mixing was never more than imperfectly realised, led for its part to a compartmentalising of sectors of activity. Conceptions of solidarity, conforming to the Islamic spirit, and to the Koranic recommendations, were however strengthened by the influence of political thought of Greek origin. 'Man is a political being by nature', the Muslim thinkers repeated after Aristotle; this implied for them that man could only exist in society, that each needed the others to survive, and that each must occupy in society the place which was his according to his aptitudes. This idea, expressed by Miskawayh in the eleventh century was taken up by Ibn Khaldūn in the nineteenth century; this shows the durability of an ideal, which always remained alive, even if it did not always appear in actual fact.

CHAPTER 6

Centres of civilisation

The successive shades of doctrine and the political and social organisation which characterised the world of Islam in the Middle Ages found their full expression in the living variety of active centres which appeared there, each with its own history and destiny, and all marked also by the play of local conditions, where we have seen the complex geographical and ethnic factors controlling the successive transformations of Islamic space. To insist now on the number and basic originality of each of these centres is certainly not to deny the authenticity of the unitary hope, which did not cease to maintain itself under the religious and social tensions of every medieval Muslim milieu. It is rather to seek, at the level of facts and their material results, some of the lessons more fitted to show us the specific character of the Islamic civilisation of this time, which was indeed animated by different currents but succeeded in integrating them into its urban settings and into its art.

1 Towns and types of historic buildings

Centres of culture developed essentially in the towns, whose rise was, as has been said, favoured by the conditions of political and economic life which prevailed from the establishment of the first empire of Islam. All cultural and artistic activity was concentrated there, and the only historic buildings of some interest outside them existed for the needs of defence or commerce; strong castles on the one hand, and on the other hand buildings destined to facilitate communications, like bridges, and above all the caravanserais used by merchants and travellers as well as by the couriers of the official post.

These towns, whether founded by the conquerors or occupying ancient sites, showed, in the medieval period, a certain number of common characteristics sufficiently definite, so that with reference to them, one could speak of an 'Islamic city'. This idea, however, which was much discussed for several years, must be qualified, because the characteristics in question here belong less to Islam as such than to the civilisation of distinctly Oriental character, which stemmed from it, and to its successive aspects in the course of time. This explains how the cities of the Umayyad period, those of the 'Abbāsid period and those of the Seljuk period showed notable differences – accentuated too by the geographical conditions prevailing here or there – within a world which in this respect was more diversified than one has often tended to say.

The first of these cities were of moderate size, and the palace of the king or governor only occupied a small space in the immediate vicinity of the great mosque, which formed the principal, often the central, element. When the 'Abbāsid empire came into being, we see appearing on the contrary ever greater conurbations for the intense commercial activity from which the palace often remained isolated. But this latter also soon came to assume sometimes colossal proportions, so as to form, at a lesser or greater distance from the city of merchants and artisans, a truly independent town, described often today by the expression 'royal city' or 'city of government'. Then a little later, after the dismemberment of the empire, the central regions, by the chances of their history, experienced an unequal prosperity, and this affected the physiognomy of cities, enclosed henceforth within a protective wall, provided with citadels, and sheltering buildings, such as colleges and monasteries, resulting from the dissociation of the primary religious role which had at first devolved uniquely on the great mosque.

Thus if there were 'Islamic' cities similar to each other, chiefly because of the place held by certain types of religious buildings which appeared with Islam and were imposed by it, these towns have also successively resembled in their structure either huge metropolises comparable to Byzantium, or fortified towns such as existed at this time in medieval Europe. The Muslim character of their inhabitants was therefore not sufficient in itself to have specific effects: what animated them was due rather to the effect of historical circumstances, which formed them differently according to places and times. Also recognisable was the influence of the political and social environment peculiar to each of the great periods, which were marked, from the beginning of Islam, sometimes by the ascendancy of a central power which sent everywhere representatives charged with maintaining order, sometimes on the contrary by the demonstrations of local militias opposing the more or less great prestige of the jurists and traditionists as well as the leaders of the mystical brotherhoods. Thus in the course of the Islamic Middle Ages there were cities whose organisation was very similar to that of contemporary western or Asiatic towns, though at the same time distinct in certain details, but there was no typical 'Islamic city' which one could contrast as such with the city of the Christian West.

The only permanent feature which seems to unite a certain number of Muslim towns of every period is without doubt the compartmentalisation of their districts by tribes, ethnic groups or religious sects. In the first camp-cities, the inhabitants were, we are told, distributed by tribes. Later, at Samarra for example, one district was specially allocated to Turkish mercenaries employed by the caliph, while another grouped together the activities of merchants and artisans. Moreover, notably in the cities of Syria, the Jews and the Christians who were not converted occupied definite and quite distinct sectors where they collected. Under Seljuk rule the same was done by the Turks of the new army, who generally established themselves in the outer suburbs of the city proper. But one sees from these few examples that the formation of these compartmentalised districts varied according to social climate and political events, so much so that, from this point of view, the physiognomy of the localities was continuously modified.

Thus there has been much discussion as to the existence or absence of a Muslim urbanism as such, and the tendency has often been to deny the existence of it. This was based on the example of certain cities, above all Syrian, where the arrangements inherited from antiquity deteriorated progressively; such were Aleppo, Damascus and Latakia, where the avenues with rectilinear porticos gave way gradually to winding commercial streets lined with shops. The circumstances which favoured such a development – one vouched for by archaeological evidence but difficult to place chronologically – remain however obscure. Indeed it seems certain that in the Umayyad period the ancient plan had at first been respected to the point of being imitated in the construction of one of those rare new Umayyad towns, whose traces have been preserved, namely that of 'Anjar on the foothills of Anti-Lebanon. But without doubt it was wrong to want to date a decline from the following era; in the absence of contrary evidence this decline may have begun only in the eleventh and twelfth centuries, when the central authority failed to ensure peace and protection in the large cities. Up to then, on the contrary, the broad main streets would have been maintained and the skilful geometrical pattern of the town plan would have been respected.

We know, moreover, to support such a hypothesis, that in the twelfth century, too, the manuals of *hisba* recommended that the footpaths of the avenues with colonnades should be kept clear, and that in the 'Abbāsid period the newly created cities of government showed in their conception a real concern for methodical organisation. This is true of the 'round city' of Baghdad, which has unfortunately vanished, and which can be reconstructed from the texts in rather different ways; the same is true of Samarra or of Raqqa in the same Iraqi province, and of cities set up in Tunisia, then in Egypt by the conquering Fātimids, such as Mansuriyya, Mahdiya and especially Cairo. Thus it cannot be said that the founders of medieval Muslim cities were not concerned about their layout, since the chronicles tell us in each of these cases of 'plans' traced in advance, and of programmes elaborated to respond to precise objectives, with the aid of engineer-geometricians, and even taking into account the astral conjunctions which would sway the destiny of the new city because of its horoscope.

But why, in these conditions, did mazes of alleyways, which can still be seen today in Fez and Damascus, come to characterise the towns of the Islamic countries? This situation can only be the result of transformations which took place gradually in the course of centuries. In fact, we have already noticed, justifiably, that the town has no status properly speaking, in Muslim law, and that the magistrate charged with the oversight of the highways has no other obligation except to enforce the rights of every person. There is no municipal authority, since the powers are concentrated in the hands of the ruler or of his representatives; there is only the private property of its inhabitants, and the role of the only 'municipal' magistrate as already indicated was to prevent a Muslim from curtailing the freedom of other Muslims, notably by obstructing free passage in the street. The idea of common utility is thus left to the appreciation of each person occupying a function, and no principle, for example, obliges the *muhtasib* to keep a street in a straight line; the only important thing is to be able to move freely. To this may be added the fact that the houses in a Muslim environment are arranged in terms of their interior space to suit the life of a family or tribe turned in on itself; it also appeared normal to set up rows of shops backing on to any sort of building concealing the façades but also ensuring for the future the revenues destined for their upkeep; we can thus understand that the architectural character of a whole complex has been rarely studied for itself. Even the large squares, more numerous in the medieval urban web than they were later, answered to a design which was practical as well as aesthetic, forming vast esplanades planned for troop reviews or games of polo, situated in the immediate vicinity of the citadel of the governor's residence, but which disappeared at the same time as the armies of horsemen.

Periods of anarchy favoured, on the other hand, the uniting of houses in protected quarters to which access could be gained at only one point, which could be shut at nightfall; this need for security has added to the effect of legal requirements and living habits to bring about the establishment of a type of living quarter in compact and irregular clusters, which were served by narrow and twisting alleyways where only pedestrians and beasts of burden passed after wheeled vehicles had been abandoned. The phenomenon is, however, only partially observed in some cities, those which aroused the interest of rulers who imposed certain building programmes on them to form the specifically royal section. Hence the manifestations which we still recognise from later times, notably in Isfahan in the Safavid period (seventeenth century), where a wonderful structured unity was conceived by Shāh 'Abbās to surround the site of his palace. On the other hand, if the rulers lost interest in a town founded before they settled in it, or if they moved their residence to a citadel as in Cairo, this was enough for the city to see its noble original plan debased by the ruin and the pillage of its most prestigious elements.

As for the buildings themselves, the first building in every town in an Islamic country was clearly the mosque, that is the 'great mosque', intended to house the gathering of the people when brought together, as they are still brought together, by the Friday mid-day Prayer. Each Muslim can in fact perform the five daily prayers wherever he wishes, even alone, whereas the Friday Prayer is obligatory as a collective Prayer. The first great mosques of historic note appeared under the Umayyad caliphs at the end of the seventh century and the very beginning of the eighth century, at the same time both in the cities created after the conquest, such as Basra, Kufa, Fustat and later, Wasit, and also in older cities Islamised, like Damascus, Aleppo and Jerusalem, without counting Medina, where a place for meeting and prayer had naturally existed in the lifetime of the Prophet, although at that time there was no permanent structure.

This great mosque newly created was in the image of the infant civilisation. As a building, it could only depend on earlier traditions and customs: thus Jean Sauvaget has shown that its first structure was an adaptation of the type of the basilica. But at the same time it showed an undeniable originality because of its specific function. It was not only a sanctuary; it was the place where the ruler – or his representative – called together the members of the community to deliver speeches, which were mostly political as well as religious. This led to the arrangement with a central bay where the ruler or his representative, leader of the Prayer, normally stood, a bay which had been enlarged on the model of an audience chamber, the side areas being reserved for the faithful who were arranged in parallel rows for the ritual Prayer. The character of power in Islam, as both spiritual and temporal, is thus reflected in the conception of the great mosque of the early periods. And even if, afterwards, the caliph was dispossessed of a large part of his powers, the various petty kings, emirs, sultans and dynasts, who later held authority, adopted an attitude identical with that of the old caliphs. The great mosque, whose structure and decor was appreciably changed, especially in Iran, from the eleventh century, preserved an interior arrangement which reserved a privileged place for the governor or prince and his entourage.

The building itself, which was generally situated in the centre of the older remodelled towns like Damascus, often took the place of a former Byzantine church, which had itself replaced a pagan sanctuary. In such a case the size of the prayer room and the adjacent courtyard corresponded to those of the previous sanctuary, and the proportions thus adopted could be imitated. However, these were only isolated phenomena, and the new buildings which came into being later or elsewhere often showed different arrangements. From another point of view, the (surface) area of the great mosque went on increasing as the towns developed, since such a meeting-place, unique for each in the early days of Islam, should have been able to contain the whole of the male inhabitants of this town, so that the area of the mosque enables one to calculate their number in some fashion. It remains clear, however, that this last procedure, difficult to carry out, is moreover only valid for cities of medium size like Cordova. The problem is much more complex when considering a metropolis like Baghdad, which was constituted by several juxtaposed urban clusters, each possessing its great mosque; this model became the rule in later periods, and led to the multiplication of mosques with a minbar, which were very often identified from then on as simple local mosques.

A place of prayer in any case since its origin, the great mosque was also very soon a place of instruction. There, in fact, the doctors brought together their disciples in a circle round them to teach them the religious sciences, essentially the sciences of tradition and of law. We are dealing with a giving of instruction more or less controlled by the authorities, from which were excluded those who held somewhat suspect doctrines, whether it was *falsafa*, rationalising Mu'tazilism or even Sūfism. But the intellectual life concentrated in the chief sanctuary of each town also tended to spread itself into the whole of the quarter surrounding the great mosque, generally a business quarter. Not only were there found in the middle of the shops a number of small oratories where less official instruction was imparted; but the crowd that pressed in on them was also harangued by preachers of various tendencies, whose activity besides could be limited, nay even forbidden, by authority when it was considered to be contrary to government policy; among these preachers there figured, alongside the Sūfis, real propagandists who were working against the established régime.

From the eleventh to the twelfth centuries, or even earlier in some towns, there next appeared, in the form of buildings, sometimes independent of the great mosque, sometimes gravitating around it, specialist establishments of instruction, especially legal instruction, called *madrasas*, 'colleges', which benefited from trust funds by means of which the professors were paid and the students maintained. In most of the towns in the Near East, these *madrasas* were built sometimes within the town walls and sometimes outside. They often owed their existence to great personages, sometimes rulers who wanted to use them to promote a definite policy; but they could also be founded by rich merchants or other unofficial persons, who were happy to favour by this means the juridico-religious school to which they belonged. The *madrasas* from about the twelfth century became an indispensable element of town life, as well as being very active intellectual and religious centres assuring the training of future scholars. However they encountered more favour in some regions and less in others. Syria, for example, was the country of choice, whereas they experienced a less important expansion in Egypt or even in Iraq, not to mention the Maghrib where they expanded more slowly. The circumstances which encouraged, or on the contrary hindered, their development still remain to be determined, although in some cases, one can already discern them.

Parallel with this development there appeared, in most of the towns, monasteries with names varying to correspond to the realities which were themselves changing. Alongside the genuine monasteries of Sūfis, where for their daily spiritual exercises members of an 'order' grouped themselves around their master, we must also mention in fact the simple hostelries which gave shelter to pilgrims more or less renouncing the world. More modest buildings also housed pious people spreading their doctrine among a small circle of initiates. These various types of buildings which doubtless existed, though in a small number, from the tenth century, multiplied from about the twelfth century, just like the *madrasas*, and it seems that in certain cases the rulers may have tried to rely on the monasteries, as on the *madrasas*, to strengthen a trend towards communal regrouping to help them reconcile public opinion and to rally goodwill.

Away from these buildings frequented by men of religion and ordinary people, for the practice of worship or instruction in religious knowledge, there generally towered the palace of the ruler or his representative. At first situated opposite the great mosque to allow direct movement from one building to another, the palace was later separated, as in

'Abbāsid Samarra or Fāṭimid Cairo, and still later moved to the centre of the citadels found in the principal towns; the 'Abbāsid empire, relatively centralised, was then broken up to give place to multiple, sometimes ephemeral, principalities, and the provincial capitals had become so many fortified places where princes, constantly warring with each other, took refuge. The palace-citadel was often far from the great mosque where the ruler only appeared on rare occasions for solemn feasts, for more often he had at his disposal his own princely oratory of greater or lesser dimensions, inside or near his apartments. This arrangement continued customs long practised in Baghdad, where the caliph hardly ever left his residential quarters, these being situated from the eleventh century within a fortified wall.

The palace traditionally comprised one part reserved for private life and another where the ruler received friends, ministers and visitors. This does not mean that every palace necessarily had an audience chamber, but each had at least a group of ceremonial apartments, used more specifically by the ruler and which were situated far from the entrance-gate; these were only reached by crossing courtyards, gardens, halls and various buildings. We have in fact seen how the ruler only appeared on few and rare occasions to those introduced privately by the chancellor with his permission, or to various dignitaries taking part in solemn audiences held weekly or fortnightly.

In more constant manner, on the contrary, within the framework of intimate receptions, there was seen the influence of rulers who were not solely preoccupied with political problems but who greatly appreciated meetings and entertainments of all kinds, both sportive and of an intellectual nature. Most often they played the role of patrons who showed favour to poets and musicians, sometimes also to the humanists and scholars more or less imbued with philosophy. Arts and letters thus found support in the royal courts. During the first centuries the caliphal capital, that is Baghdad, or for a brief period Samarra, was almost the unique centre of culture; there, the poets, even natives of distant provinces, came to present their panegyrics; there, too, artists and artisans came together to work at building and decorating sumptuous buildings as well as at manufacturing objects and robes; and finally it was there, too, that scholars and writers of the highest repute met. Afterwards the dissolution of the empire contributed to the scattering of these centres; not only did the great cities of Spain, of the Maghrib and of Egypt take on this role, but also the provincial capitals of Syria, with the Hamdānids of Aleppo for example, and the cities of Iran and Transoxiana with the Samānid, Būyid or Ghaznavid princes as well as the Seljuk sultans, not to mention the localities ultimately destined to become the capitals of the Zangids, Ayyūbids or Seljuks of Rūm.

Artists and artisans, musicians, poets and essayists thus lived in large measure on the favours or orders accorded them by large and small dynasties. The importance of patronage in Islamic civilisation is a feature which one cannot overemphasise. Art and secular culture were almost entirely subject to the authorities. There were some writers, however, who preserved their independence, as well as most men of religion, for they had, as we have seen, their own means of subsistence thanks to their personal fortunes, or to the profession they practised in addition, and this allowed them to write and sometimes teach in their own home without needing to beg for subsidies. Some poets – but this was rare – were also able to preserve a certain liberty. In general, however, it is very clear that the works produced by these various people, even when they did not receive official support, were not popular in character; they were intended for a class of rich people of mixed origin where the cultivated élite rubbed shoulders with upstarts of low extraction, but whose common desire was to live apart from the crowd whom they despised.

2 Islamic Art

We have seen earlier what were the complex bases of such a culture, religious or humanist, as far as one can define it in its literary manifestations. The art which appeared for its part in the sumptuous buildings, as well as in the indispensable furnishings of the daily life of the great, had it analogous sources? Not in the same way, for in this domain Arab tradition was almost non-existent, with the exception of South Arabia which does not seem to have exercised a great influence on the Hijaz. The architectural art which appeared during the first centuries, especially in Syria and in Iraq, for in Arabia its expression remained limited, is found in fact in the continuation of the arts which had previously flourished in the regions conquered by Islam. The plans of the first great mosques are explained by the imitation of plans in vogue in late antiquity for various uses, as much as by the needs of the ceremonial of the Friday Prayer and its solemn address. The *mihrab*, for example, the niche where the imām stands to lead the collective prayer, has been interpreted as an apse reduced in size, although other origins could have been put forward, and although, afterwards, Muslims might have seen in it above all the symbol of Islamic monotheism. It was in Syria after all that this plan of the great mosque emerged, and it was in the interior of the peribolos of an ancient temple of Zeus still retaining its temenos that the new Islamic edifice was inserted. In all probability the other great mosques, including the one at Medina rebuilt in the Umayyad era, were modelled more or less exactly on the Damascus model.

For its part, the 'Dome of the Rock', built on the esplanade of the old temple in Jerusalem, drew on the same type of heritage. This was a building of a particular kind, a sort of reliquary, sheltering the rock from which the Prophet was reputed to have been taken up on his 'night journey' and which was also bound up with memories of Abraham. This famous building constructed for a purpose which does not appear very clear to us today, was, more than any other, a replica of neighbouring Christian buildings, but it was not imitated afterwards. Although certain mausoleums or commemorative buildings might be connected with it, it must be seen rather as the end of a tradition or a transitional form.

In any case it is a witness to the force of the influences which affected the Islamic architecture of early times.

The civil buildings of this epoch are for their part less well known, which makes it difficult to establish their dependence on ancient buildings. However, the audience chamber, which in the majority of princely residences formed an essential element shows clearly that here too a tradition existed which was perpetuated. Thus a palace like that of Mshatta in Transjordan, which fits perfectly into the totality of residential buildings known in Umayyad 'greater Syria', could have been at one time claimed by the art of previous epochs, while the recent excavations of an Umayyad foundation like Anjar made it possible to find again here the faithful transposition of a classical city with its axial streets and avenues with colonnades.

As to the decoration of all these buildings, whether religious or secular, it was very close to that of classical Byzantine buildings. This is true of the mosaics which adorned, and still adorn, the walls of the porticos of the great mosque of Damascus, panels of admirable composition, which, according to tradition, had been executed by local artists trained before Islam, if not indeed by artists brought from the Byzantine empire. This is also true of the mosaics which adorn different parts of the Dome of the Rock, and which were inspired either by Sassanid motifs or by stylised Byzantine motifs. This is true again of the external sculptures of the palace of Mshatta, of the statues and stucco panels of the palace of Khirbat al-Mafjar near Jericho, and finally of certain frescoes of the palace of Kasr al-Hayr in Syria, frescoes in which one recognises traces of Parthian art or of Greco-Roman iconography.

Islamic art, however, developed very quickly certain features of this décor, notably an ornamentation which accentuates the stylisation of floral motifs, accords a new place to purely geometrical elements, and restricts or even suppresses representations of living beings. From this point of view the decoration of the Umayyad period forms a transition between the art of late antiquity and that of the heyday of the Islamic period.

Afterwards the classical heritage became stultified, until it was no longer recognisable. The distinctive Islamic stamp of architectural forms was emphasised as ancient models were forgotten and new local influences made themselves felt. The geometric decoration spread in all the provinces despite regional variants which appeared here and there; it became associated more and more with a new type of abstract ornament derived from diverse forms of calligraphy; and the figured representations totally proscribed in a country like the Maghrib, where certain prophetic traditions concerning these were strictly observed, remained however limited in use, despite the vogue enjoyed by miniatures chiefly in Irano-Turkish countries. Thus a true Islamic art was formed whose unity could not be questioned, and whose decorative style appealed more to intelligence than to sensibility.

But despite this spirit which always animated it, this art did not cease to evolve in the course of centuries, as it reflected successive or simultaneous aspects of the civilisation which it expressed. The most characteristic example is without doubt that of the great mosques which presented, in Iran from the eleventh century, then in Anatolia a little later, new plans appropriate to the Persian and Turkish types of this essentially Islamic building. The appearance at almost the same moment of other distinctive architectural creations, in response to the need for increasing numbers of buildings to shelter the *madrasas* and monasteries, is another example of this. The face of the cities was thus transformed, while these various buildings experienced local variations corresponding to the taste and building techniques peculiar to each region.

Thus there were many elements of observation hardly touched on here, which would contribute to place the artistic manifestations among the evidence revealing traditions which were evolving gradually in the course of time and were assuring the individuality of the different centres of civilisation existing in the world of Islam. The fact has often claimed the attention of historians, who have studied the arts in question by emphasising, for some years, their diversity, as well as the strictly 'national' links of this or that school. Nevertheless it does not seem that they have succeeded in giving it its right place amid other factors, as numerous in their influence in this domain as in that of thought, and also as dependent on historic as well as on religious realities.

It remains for us, then, to underline a multiplicity of aspects which vary with each centre and which as regards architecture, as well as the sumptuary and furnishing arts, join up with the Muslim vocation of buildings or objects, which their inscriptions often made sacred in this sense. And we must not forget that the spread of Islamic culture to the countries of the west also happened from the different centres to which its various manifestations had spread out. If it is not in our remit to deal, even briefly, with the modalities of this influence nor the ways which it has assumed, this influence remains one of the best proofs of the vitality of a civilisation which stirred up reactions in medieval Europe which were sometimes contradictory, according to the aspect of them which was presented, but which continued none the less for their part to evolve, following their own laws, until the new encounters of the modern and contemporary period.

Conclusion

Religious movements, political ambitions, social and indeed socio-economic tensions and regional peculiarities all go to make up the elements which are found closely interwoven with the principal events which affected the medieval world of Islam. If they never ceased in the course of centuries to combine in different forms, they were very apparent from the earliest years of Islam. Thus the phenomenon of the conquests, explained basically by the existence of a new religion with universalist tendency, would have been unable to generate itself had not the human reservoir, Arabia, long since begun to provide neighbouring countries with new populations. Similarly, in the early days, the necessities of government and the exigencies of Islam combined to form an original autocratic régime tempered by the control of tribal chiefs and taking on an undeniably religious character. As a result, successive régimes were always careful to affirm their respect for Islam, even presenting themselves as the only ones true to the legacy of the Prophet, which does not show however that this preoccupation was the determining motive of their promoters, who were also carried along by their personal designs and capable of exploiting all the latent discontent.

The celebrated 'Abbāsid 'revolution', which in 750 brought to power the descendants of al-'Abbās and put an end to the Umayyad caliphate is one of the best examples of this. The 'Abbāsid princes, who fermented it, succeeded in obtaining the support of the Shi'ite movement by presenting themselves as members of the Prophet's family, designated by their descent to succeed him; they regarded themselves as the only legitimate chiefs and the only ones capable of leading the community down the right road, which their Umayyad predecessors, accused of impiety, in their opinion had never done. But not content with this single argument they also exploited the resentment of those *mawāli*, Iranians and Mesopotamians, who had not found in the Umayyad caliph's entourage the position and the consideration they had hoped for. Finally they seized power in such a way that they have been regarded as mere ambitious adventurers. If in fact religious and social elements predominated among the factors contributing to their success, what were their convictions? Did they simply make use of Shi'ism, which they repelled some time after their victory, or did they share the idea, or some of the ideas, of the movement? It is impossible to say. At least we can try to determine the relative importance of the factors of their victory and in particular to try to discover the ethnic and social origin of the leaders who supported them.

In the same way the régime set up by the Fātimid caliphs in Ifriqiya in 909 was a régime which pretended to follow the 'real' right way by giving power to the 'real' successors of the Prophet. It is none the less true that some doubt hangs over the genealogy of the first of these caliphs in whom some historians see a propagandist pure and simple, who had no connection with the family of 'Ali, nor do we know what was the origin of the later caliphs whose claims were contested by the opponents of this régime. We know on the other hand that the Fātimid régime, in order to become established, enjoyed the support of a Berber tribe, that of the Kutāma, without whom it would never have come into being: what was this tribe's objective – to restore the true Islam or to exercise its own power?

What was valid for the Fātimid régime was also valid for the numerous rebellions which prompt one to ask if the deep-seated reason was the religious conviction of their followers, the personal ambition of their leaders or the particularly unfavourable position of a social group. We have already seen that in medieval Islam opposition to all established rule nearly always expressed itself by the appearance of 'heresies'. In the early days in Iran, those in revolt sided with non-Islamic Iranian doctrines; there was the case of a person called al-Muqanna', the 'veiled', and later on, at the turn of the eighth and ninth centuries, that of the rebel Bābak, who for some time was a follower of Shi'ism, and for others a reincarnation of the ancient prophets, while directing an action of very marked social character. Subsequently the same rebels placed themselves instead under the banner of an Islamic 'heresy' and no longer outside Islam: so it was in the case of the Zanj, whose leader claimed to be descended from 'Ali. But the question always remains of knowing whether the underlying motive was the discontent of a population, or of a social group, or the effect of a religious propaganda which sought in preference to carry with it the underprivileged.

This last explanation is certainly valid in the case of the Ismā'īli undertakings, whether it be the Carmathians of Syria or Arabia or again the Fātimids. But concerning a revolt as localised as that of the Zanj, we must proceed with greater prudence; these slaves, forced to work in unhealthy swamps, preoccupied by their material state, doubtless only had the most summary knowledge of the ideology to which their leader professed his adherence, and the latter was probably influenced by opportunism rather than by deep convictions. Social tensions must not be neglected as far as we know them. They are without doubt at the origin of the movement of these governors of Sistan called Saffārids after their first representative who was a coppersmith to trade. But the Shi'ite claimants were active in the region of the Caspian on the one hand and in Yemen on the other; and it appears that it was above all the remoteness of these countries, mountainous as well and so more difficult of access, which prompted them to choose these places in which to settle. As for what happened in Muslim Spain, this was the result both of the class rivalries which divided the Arabs in the east and of the particularism of the inhabitants of this peripheral province, without there being any ideology which really affected the separatist movement of the Umayyad emirs of al-Andalus.

The particularism of the peripheral regions is indeed a factor to which particular attention must be paid, since it was in large measure at the root of the splitting up of the primitive Islamic empire and of the secession of various provinces, beginning with Muslim Spain and continuing through the Maghrib (Rustamids, Idrīsids, Aghlabids) and through other regions like Egypt or Transoxiana and Khorasan. To this particularism was added the situation created in the east and also in the west by the invasions of nomadic elements, or simply the intrusion of foreigners picked for their military qualities. Acclimatised foreigners were, for example, the Turks commanded by Sebuktigin who became the Ghaznavids. These Ghaznavids, well known for having undertaken the conquest of India, also played an important role in taking up the fight against Shi'ism in Iran and supporting the efforts of the caliphs of Baghdad in their struggle against the powerful Būyid emirs with Imāmite sympathies. The position they adopted on the doctrinal level – for reasons which remain to be explained – had important consequences for the political development of the Islamic east. The Seljuks, on the contrary, were invaders who, not content with dominating Iran, appeared in Iraq, obtaining in 1045 investiture from the caliph, who thus got rid of the undesirable Būyid emirs. New masters of the eastern regions, the Seljuk sultans set themselves up as the champions of Sunnism and on this ground gained the title of 'kings of the east and of the west'; they carried on the war against the Fātimids of Syria and reopened the road of the Pilgrimage. No one can tell how sincere their Sunnism was, but what is important is that they could not claim to dominate such a vast empire without taking up a stance on religious questions.

Even more striking perhaps are the examples of the states set up in the Maghrib first by the Almoravids, then by the

Almohads. Both had a quite distinctive religious complexion, and it was in a spirit of reform – set moreover within the framework of Sunnism – that the newcomers, nomads from the Sahara on the one hand, Berber mountaineers on the other, founded empires which embraced what remained of Muslim Spain. Contrary to what happened in the east, ideology officially played its role in the organisation of régimes, whose appearance had none the less been demanded by the irruption of new ethnic elements.

Religious problems and personal ambitions were still inextricably tied up with each other when we consider in the east the career of the rulers who undertook the struggles against the Crusaders. Was it as a result of piety and conviction that Nūr al-dīn, for example, favoured the men of religion belonging to the Hanafite and Shāfi'ite schools and had *madrasas* and monasteries built? Or rather, did he seek above all to increase his prestige and to strengthen his power by mobilising all his energies to fight the infidels? Along the same lines the personality of Salāh al-dīn or Saladin, has been recently questioned. It has been noticed indeed that this ruler, from the moment when he became the heir of his former master, Nūr al-dīn, was careful not to undertake any action against the Crusaders, but engaged in various expeditions against Muslim kinglets, his rivals, in such a way as to strengthen and increase his Syrian kingdom, while the men of religion were demanding the recapture of Jerusalem. And it was only after he had succeeded in his various warlike enterprises that he decided to listen to the lawyers and cadis and to direct his attention against the Crusaders, whom he crushed at Hattin. Was the counter-crusade, as has been thought until now, really his one aim, or was this only one aspect of power politics? It is difficult to answer such a question, which in fact creates a false problem. At the period we are considering, the defence of Islam against the Franks represented the prime preoccupation of Muslims, and the best way to acquire prestige was to commit oneself to this struggle. Consequently it is wrong to think that Saladin was indifferent to this cause or that he pushed it into second place; political realism alone could have led him to postpone his attack on the Crusaders so as to reinforce his own power; but as for sounding his inmost convictions, no one would claim to do this.

Equally difficult to understand is the nature of internal tensions in a town. There too social and religious problems are in fact closely intertwined. Confrontations between rival bands or between popular groups often have a religious aspect. This is what happened at Baghdad, in particular during the Būyid period (945–1059), and again at the beginning of the Seljuk period. During the first period we see the Sunnites and Shi'ites confronting each other, then, during the second, the Ash'arites and the Hanbalites. But the Hanbalites generally recruited their followers from the common people, while the Shi'ites were chiefly supported by the rich merchants of the town. Other confrontations, for example, those between the people of Baghdad and al-Ma'mūn's army between 813 and 815, were not only provoked by the effects of the personal rivalry between the two sons of Hārūn al-Rashīd. Sometimes it has been suggested that there was hostility between Arab and Iranian elements. In reality it would seem to have been about something quite different; the religious politics of al-Ma'mūn, which did not follow the traditional line either doctrinally or in its conception of the caliphate, was beginning to meet in Iraq with a hostility which drove the lower classes to support with violence the cause of his predecessor.

In a still clearer manner, the clashes which took place in the twelfth century in the towns of Syria, which had been brought by the Seljuks into the sphere of the 'Abbāsid caliphate, were essentially of a politico-religious order. The Ismā'īlis, despite their tenacity, were reduced to silence, sometimes brutally, since in Damascus in particular, they were massacred without pity. But the efforts used by certain notables, sometimes men of religion and magistrates, to control cities where central power was hardly to be seen any more, for example in northern Syria or the coastal regions, corresponded both to class interests and to ideological preoccupations at a period of difficult transition from a Shi'ite to a Sunnite régime.

Each event, each movement, whether a revolt with dynastic implications or an internal confrontation, must therefore be strictly analysed, lest we prejudge in advance the motivation or the dominant causes. The history of Islam from this viewpoint presents particularly complex problems due to two essential reasons. On the one hand the Islamic religion does not present itself as a simple spiritual doctrine but conditions all the activities of life – religious, moral, social and political – at the heart of the empire which historical circumstances had subjected to the one Law associated with this doctrine. On the other hand, the social balance was continually at the mercy of the arrival of new elements of population, whether they were servile mercenaries or conquerors come from their distant steppes. But the attachment to Islam, and to the liturgical language which had become the cultural language, maintained a deeper unity than could have been thought possible in this very mixed totality, always ready to carve itself up, and which remained, despite all the divisions and all the schisms, an Arab and Islamic world. Only the 'modern' period, thought of as beginning in the sixteenth century but of which there were signs from the thirteenth century, saw the setting-up of cultural regions where the Arabic language was no longer the only literary vehicle and where the big problems showed themselves from that time under slightly different aspects.

Thus, when confining himself to the 'classical' period of Islam, the historian, without in any way challenging the study of events with which he finds himself at first confronted, must appear as a man curious about many different things. That is to say, he must be a historian of the Islamic religion as such, and of the doctrines at once theological, legal and political which it covered, at the same time as being a historian of the Islamic civilisation under its multiple intellectual and material aspects, and a historian of the early world of Islam, originally composite, as well as of the expansion and ultimate transformation which this world, always becoming more diverse, eventually came to experience. The questions presenting themselves to him are those encountered by every historian, but he must be constantly aware of their religious aspect in dealing with a world where first of all one must know to what extent religious ideology has demanded, inspired, or conditioned the development of society and of the states. Different positions, sometimes even violently opposed to each other, have been taken up by students of Islam faced with this question in each of their inquiries. Other responses have been provided by Islam itself, claiming often, even today, to regulate the entire behaviour of those who profess it, whether in private or public life, to the point that some Muslims do not even admit that their actions could be other than religiously motivated. There is thus a basic question there on which orientalists, and often, too, Muslims themselves, are not always in agreement and which the historian must study in all its aspects; it is in putting this question that he is most often led to ask whether there is such a thing as Islamic thought, an Islamic culture, an Islamic art, an Islamic social order, an Islamic economy, an Islamic civilisation. To these interrogations which are always pending, the response is sometimes by specious or sterile discussions, marred by political implications since the awakening of nationalism, but which cannot be avoided; but to these interrogations, as we have tried to show, an authentic historical perspective, setting out from the facts themselves, brings fruitful clarification.

Bibliography

ABBREVIATIONS

EI[1], *EI*[2] *Encyclopaedia of Islam*, 1st and 2nd editions
REI *Revue des études islamiques*

REFERENCE MATERIAL AND GENERAL WORKS

Encyclopaedia of Islam, 1st edn, Leiden, 1913–42; 2nd edn, Leiden, 1954 continuing (has reached K); J. Sauvaget, *Introduction to the History of the Muslim East: a Bibliographical Guide* (based on the second French edition), Berkeley, 1965; C. E. Bosworth, *The Islamic Dynasties*, Edinburgh, 1967; J. D. Pearson, *Index Islamicus 1906–1955: a Catalogue of Articles on Islamic Subjects in Periodicals, etc.*, Cambridge, 1958 (continuing with supplementary volumes); *Abstracta Islamica*, regular supplement to the *Revue des études islamiques* (Paris); 'Survey of Periodicals' (quarterly) in *The Muslim World* (Hartford, Conn.); L. Binder (ed.), *The Study of the Middle East: Research and Scholarship in the Humanities and the Social Sciences*, New York, 1976 (deals solely with the Islamic Middle East; has extensive bibliographies).

H. A. R. Gibb, *Islam* (first published as *Mohammedanism: an Historical Survey*, London, 1949); A. Guillaume, *Islam*, Harmondsworth, 1954; Fazlur Rahman, *Islam*, 2nd edn, Chicago, 1979; R. C. Martin, *Islam: a Cultural Perspective*, Englewood Cliffs, 1982; D. Sourdel, *L'Islam* and *Histoire des Arabes*, Paris, 1976; M.

Gaudefroy-Demombynes, *Muslim Institutions*, London, 1950; D. and J. Sourdel, *La Civilisation de l'Islam classique*, Paris, 1976; C. Brockelmann, *History of the Islamic Peoples*, London, 1949; P. M. Holt, A. K. S. Lambton and B. Lewis (eds), *The Cambridge History of Islam*, 2 vols, Cambridge 1970; B. Lewis, *Islam in History: Ideas, Men and Events in the Middle East*, London, 1973; P. K. Hitti, *History of the Arabs*, 10th edn, London, 1970; F. E. Peters, *Allah's Commonwealth: a History of Islam in the Near East, 600–1100*, New York, 1973 (emphasises intellectual history); W. Montgomery Watt, *The Majesty that was Islam, the Islamic World, 661–1100*, London, 1974.

Chapter 1 Islam – a monotheistic and universal religion

On Islam and its teachings there are accounts in the general works listed above; in French over 350 pages are devoted to 'the message of Muhammad' in M. Gaudefroy-Demombynes, *Mahomet*, Paris, 1957, 1969; also relevant is A. J. Wensinck, *The Muslim Creed*, Cambridge, 1932. An important discussion of the problem of Muhammad's personality and activity is M. Rodinson, 'Bilan des études mohammadiennes', *Revue historique*, 129 (1963), 169–220, with comments on other works; also R. Blachère, *Le Problème de Mahomet*, Paris, 1952; W. Montgomery Watt, *Muhammad at Mecca* and *Muhammad at Medina*, Oxford, 1953, 1956; F. Gabrieli, *Muhammad and the Conquests of Islam*, London, 1968.

On the relations between Islam and the other monotheistic religions there is no recent study. One may consult: R. Bell, *The Origin of Islam in its Christian Environment*, London, 1926; C. C. Torrey, *The Jewish Foundation of Islam*, New York, 1933; T. Andrae, *Les Origines de l'islam et le christianisme*, French tr., Paris, 1955; Y. Moubarac, *Abraham dans le Coran*, Paris, 1958: G. Parrinder, *Jesus in the Qur'ān*, London, 1965.

On the possible influence of Judaeo-Christianity see: H. J. Schoeps, *Theologie und Geschichte des Judenchristentums*, Tübingen, 1949. Recently extremely dubious attempts have been made either to connect Islam with a judaising messianism (P. Crone and M. Cook, *Hagarism, the Making of the Islamic World*, Cambridge, 1977) or to discover in the Qur'an traces of an archaic Christianity (G. Lüling, *Über den Ur-Qur'ān*, Erlangen, 1974).

On the conquests see the general accounts by D. Sourdel in R.

Folz, *De l'Antiquité au Moyen Age*, Paris, 1973; in the *Cambridge History of Islam* and in the above-mentioned work of Gabrieli.

On the situation at the beginning of the conquests see especially M. A. Shaban, *Islamic History, A.D. 600–750 (A.H. 132), a New Interpretation*, Cambridge, 1971.

On the subject peoples (*dhimmīs*) in general: A. Fattal, *Le Statut légal des non-musulmans en pays d'islam*, Beirut, 1958. On the fiscal organisation: F. Løkkegaard, *Islamic Taxation in the Classic Period*, Copenhagen, 1950; D. C. Dennett, *Conversion and the Poll-tax in Early Islam*, Cambridge (Mass.), 1950.

On the literary movements: H. A. R. Gibb, *Arabic Literature, an Introduction*, 2nd (revised) edn, Oxford, 1963; R. A. Nicholson, *A Literary History of the Arabs*, 2nd edn, Cambridge, 1930.

Chapter 2 The medieval Islamic world

On the problems of nomadism and urbanisation see especially X. de Planhol, *Les Fondements géographiques de l'histoire de l'Islam*, Paris, 1968 (with the bibliography); also W. Marçais, 'L'islamisme et la vie urbaine', in *Articles et conférences*, Paris, 1961. To be noted is: Cl. Cahen, 'Nomades et sédentaires dans le monde musulman du milieu du Moyen Age', in D. S. Richards (ed.), *Islamic Civilisation, 950–1150*, Oxford, 1973; and in the same volume: C. E. Bosworth, 'The Barbarian Invasions: the Coming of the Turks into the Islamic World'; and R. Le Tourneau, 'Nouvelles orientations des Berbères d'Afrique du Nord, 950–1150'.

On the evolution of the principal cities see *Encyclopaedia of Islam*, 2nd edn, articles: Baghdad, Dimashk (Damascus), Fas (Fez), Fustat, Halab (Aleppo), al-Kāhira (Cairo). Note the studies of J. Sauvaget, *Alep*, Paris, 1940, and L. Torres Balbás, *Ciudades hispano-musulmanas*, Madrid, n.d. (1970). See also A. H. Hourani and S. M. Stern (eds), *The Islamic City*, Oxford, 1970; and E. Wirth, 'Die orientalische Stadt' in *Saeculum*, 26 (1975), 45–94.

On pre-Islamic Arabia, in addition to the works on Muhammad by W. Montgomery Watt, mentioned under chapter 1, see M. Rodinson, 'L'Arabie avant l'Islam' in *Encyclopédie de la Pléiade, Histoire universelle*, ii (Paris, 1957), 3–36; also I. Goldziher, *Muslim Studies*, i, London, 1967.

Economic problems have attracted attention for some years; see Cl. Cahen, 'L'histoire économique et sociale de l'Orient musulman médiéval', in *Studia islamica*, iii (1955), 93–116, and various studies in the *Journal of the Economic and Social History of the Orient* (Leiden). The recent general account by E. Ashtor, *A Social and Economic History of the Near East in the Medieval Age*, London, 1976, is an interesting attempt, but somewhat premature, and it is based on preliminary studies themselves often questionable (in particular his own *Histoire des prix et des salaires dans l'Orient médiéval*, Paris, 1969. Similarly M. Lombard, *The Golden Age of Islam*, Amsterdam, 1975 (originally published as *L'Islam dans sa première grandeur*, Paris, 1971), raised important problems, but should be used with caution. A series of studies, dealing mainly with the different regions of the Islamic world, has been brought together in *Handbuch der Orientalistik* (ed. B. Spuler), I. Abteilung, VI. Band, VI. Abschnitt, *Wirtschaftsgeschichte des vorderen Orients in islamischer Zeit*, Leiden, 1977.

On commerce: W. Heyd, *Histoire du commerce du Levant au Moyen Age*, French tr., Leipzig, 1885 (reprinted); Y. Labib, *Handelsgeschichte Aegypten in Spätmittelalter*, Wiesbaden, 1965; D. S. Richards (ed.), *Islam and the Trade of Asia*, Oxford, 1970; G. F. Hourani, *Arab Seafaring in the Indian Ocean*, Beirut, 1963. On commercial organisation: A. L. Udovitch, *Partnership and Profit in Medieval Islam*, Princeton, 1970. On banking techniques: the recent account by E. Ashtor, 'Banking Instruments between the Muslim East and the Christian West', in *Journal of European Economic History* (Rome), i (1972), 553–73, as well as the remarks of M. Rodinson, *Islam and Capitalism*, London, 1974. On the Geniza of Cairo: S. D. Goitein, *A Mediterranean Society*, vol. i, *Economic Foundations*, Berkeley-Los Angeles, 1967.

On the markets: P. Chalmeta, *El señor del zoco en España*, Madrid, 1973; and *EI*[2], article: Hisba. On the suqs and bazaars there are numerous regional studies of an archaeological or geographical character. See in particular: E. Wirth, 'Zum Problem des Bazars', *Der Islam*, 51 (1974), 203–60 and 52 (1975), 6–46. On the Jewish merchants see the recent account by E. Ashtor, 'Aperçus sur les Radhanites', *Revue suisse d'histoire*, 27 (1977), 245–75 (with references to previous studies).

CHAPTER 3 ASPECTS OF ISLAMIC DOCTRINE

On Islam as a religion and the elaboration of its teachings the two basic works, apart from I. Goldziher, *Introduction to Islamic Theology and Law*, Princeton, 1981 (translated from his *Vorlesungen*, 2nd edn, Heidelberg, 1925, and now out-of-date on some points), are: H. Laoust, *Les schismes dans l'Islam*, Paris, 1965, and W. Montgomery Watt, *The Formative Period of Islamic Thought*, Edinburgh, 1973.

On law: J. Schacht, *An Introduction to Islamic Law*, Oxford, 1964 (with a detailed bibliography); N. J. Coulson, *A History of Islamic Law*, Edinburgh, 1964. H. Laoust, *Le Traité de droit d'ibn Qudama*, is an example of a Hanbalite treatise.

On the problems of methodology one may consult A. Turki, *Polémiques entre Ibn Hazm et Bagi sur les principes de la loi musulmane*, Algiers, 1975; and for a later period H. Laoust, *Contribution à une étude de la méthodologie canonique de Taki-al-din Ahmad b. Taimiya*, Cairo, 1939. On education (mainly legal): G. Makdisi, *The Rise of Colleges: Institutions of Learning in Islam and the West*, Edinburgh, 1981.

On the social role of the jurists: H. Laoust, 'Le hanbalisme sous le califat de Bagdad', *REI*, 27 (1959), 67–128; also H. Halm, *Die Ausbreitung der safi'itischen Schule*, Wiesbaden, 1974.

On the science of traditions (Hadīth): A. Guillaume, *The Traditions of Islam*, Oxford, 1924; I. Goldziher, *Muslim Studies* (ed. S. M. Stern), ii, London, 1971.

On theology in particular: L. Gardet and M. M. Anawati, *Introduction à la théologie musulmane*, Paris, 1948, is still valuable. On the earliest discussions: W. Montgomery Watt, *Free Will and Predestination in Early Islam*, London, 1948; *EI*[2], article: Kadariyya (J. van Ess); J. van Ess, *Zwischen Hadīt und Theologie: Studien zum Entstehen prädestinatianischer Überlieferung*, Berlin, 1975. The recently discovered works of the Qadi 'Abd al-Jabbār have been the subject of several scattered studies (in particular by R. M. Frank and D. Gimaret) and of two books: G. F. Hourani, *Islamic Rationalism, the Ethics of 'Abd al-Jabbār*; J. R. T. M. Peters, *God's Created Speech*, Leiden, 1976 (with appropriate bibliography).

On Ash'arism: R. J. McCarthy, *The Theology of al-Ash/arī*, Beirut, 1953; M. Allard, *Le Problème des attributs divins dans la doctrine d'al-As'arī et de ses premiers grands disciples*, Beirut, 1965.

On traditionalism: *EI*[2], articles: Ahmad b. Hanbal, Hanābila (H. Laoust); G. Makdisi, *Ibn 'Aqīl et la résurgence de l'islam traditionaliste au XI*[e] *siècle*, Damascus, 1963, and 'L'islam hanbalisant', *REI*, 42 (1974, 211–44 and 43 (1975), 45–76.

On Shī'ism: C. Van Arendonk, *Les Débuts de l'imamat zaydite du Yémen*, French tr., Leiden, 1960; W. Madelung, *Der Imām al-Qāsim ibn Ibrāhīm und die Glaubenslehre der Zaiditen*, Berlin, 1965;

D. M. Donaldson, *The Shi'ite Religion*, London, 1933; D. Sourdel, 'L'imamisme vu par le cheikh al-Mufid', *REI*, 40 (1972), 217–96; H. Corbin, *Histoire de la philosophie islamique*, Paris, 1964 (only to 1198); B. Lewis, *The Origins of Ismā'īlism*, Cambridge, 1940; M. G. S. Hodgson, *The Order of Assassins*, The Hague, 1955; W. Madelung, 'Fatimiden und Bahrainqarmaten', *Der Islam*, 34 (1958), 34–88, and 'Das Imamat in der frühen ismailitischen Lehren', *Der Islam*, 37 (1961), 43–135; Y. Marquet, *La Philosophie des Ihwan al-safa*, Lille, 1973.

On Sufism: A. J. Arberry, *Sufism, an Account of the Mystics of Islam*, London, 1950; A. Schimmel, *Mystical Dimensions of Islam*, Chapel Hill, 1975; L. Massignon, *The Passion of al-Hallaj, Mystic and Martyr of Islam*, 4 vols, London, 1981 (translated from the second French edition, 1975); J. van Ess, *Die Gedankenwelt des Harit al-Muhasibi*, Bonn, 1961; R. J. McCarthy, *Freedom and Fulfilment*, Boston, 1980 (translations from al-Ghazali, with introduction); W. Montgomery Watt, *Muslim Intellectual*, Edinburgh, 1963; H. Laoust, *La Politique de Gazali*, Paris, 1970.

On philosophy: F. Rosenthal, *The Classical Heritage in Islam*, London, 1975; M. Fakhry, *History of Islamic Philosophy*, New York, 1970; *EI*[2], article: Falsafa (R. Arnaldez); D. M. Donaldson, *Studies in Muslim Ethics*, London, 1953.

On the literati: Ch. Pellat, *Le milieu basrien et la formation de Gahiz*, Paris, 1953; and *The Life and Works of Jahiz*, London, 1969; G. Lecomte, *Ibn Qutayba, l'homme, son oeuvre, ses idées*, Damascus, 1965; M. Arkoun, 'L'humanisme arabe aux IVe-Xe siècles', *Studia Islamica*, 14 (1961), 73–108, and 15 (1961), 63–88; M. Bergé, *Essai sur la personnalité morale et intellectuelle d'Abū Ḥayyān al-Tauhidi*, Lille, 1974.

Chapter 4 Islam and the political order

Political thought and order have not been the subject of many studies. On political institutions see: E. Tyan, *Institution du droit public musulman*, I: *Le califat*, Paris, 1954; II: *Sultanat et califat*, Paris, 1957; D. Sourdel, *Le Vizirat 'abbāside de 749 à 936*, 2 vols, Damascus, 1959–60; E. Tyan, *Histoire de l'organisation judiciaire en pays de l'Islam*, Leiden, 1960.

See also: E. I. J. Rosenthal, *Political Thought in Medieval Islam*, Cambridge, 1958, and 'The Role of the State in Islam: Theory and the Medieval Practice', *Der Islam*, 50 (1973), 2–27; W. Montgomery Watt, *Islamic Political Thought, the Basic Concepts*, Edinburgh, 1968; Ch. Pellat, *Ibn al-Muqaffa' 'conseilleur' du calife*, Paris, 1976. H. A. R. Gibb, *Studies on the Civilization of Islam*, London, 1962, has articles relevant to the subjects of this and other chapters.

Though it deals with a later period, recourse may also be had to: H. Laoust, *Essai sur les doctrines . . . d'Ibn Taimiya*, Cairo, 1939.

For consultation: al-Mawardi, *Les Statuts gouvernementaux*, Algiers, 1915 (French tr. by E. Fagnan); H. Laoust, 'La pensée et l'action politiques d'al-Mawardi', *REI*, 36 (1968), 11–92; Nizam al-Mulk, *The Book of Government or Rules for Kings*, London, 1960 (Eng. tr. by H. Darke).

Chapter 5 Islam and the social order

There have been hardly any systematic studies of the social structure of Islamic countries in medieval times. See the material provided by: R. Levy, *The Social Structure of Islam*, Cambridge, 1955 (a revision of a work published in 1933 under a different title); G. E. von Grunebaum, *Medieval Islam, a Study in Cultural Orientation*, Chicago, 1946, esp. 170–220; W. Montgomery Watt, *Islam and the Integration of Society*, London, 1961; Cl. Cahen, 'L'évolution sociale du monde musulman face à celle du monde chrétien jusque au XIIe siècle', *Cahiers de civilisation médiévale*, i (1958), 431–63, and ii (1959), 37–51; D. and J. Sourdel, *La Civilisation de l'Islam classique* (above), esp. 431–66; L. Gardet, *Les Hommes de l'Islam*, Paris, 1977, 95–117. See also M. Rodinson, 'Histoire économique et sociale des classes sociales dans le monde musulman', in M. A. Cook (ed.), *Studies in the Economic History of the Middle East*, London, 1970, 139–55.

On social movements: E. Ashtor, *Social and Economic History of the Middle East* (above); and 'Républiques urbaines dans le Proche-Orient à l'époque des croisades?' *Cahiers de civilisation médiévale*, 18 (1975), 117–31; Cl. Cahen, 'Mouvements populaires et autonomisme urbaine dans l'Asie musulmane au Moyen Age', *Arabica*, 5 (1958), 229–50 and 6 (1959), 251–6, 233–65; A. Havemann, *Ri'āsa und qadā'*, Freiburg im Breisgau, 1975; A. Popovic, *La Révolte des esclaves en Iraq au IIIe–IXe siècle*, Paris, 1976; on the problem of corporations: Hourani and Stern (eds), *The Islamic City* (above).

For a later period: I. M. Lapidus, *Muslim Cities in the later Middle Ages*, Cambridge (Mass.), 1967; A. K. S. Lambton, *Islamic Society in Persia*, London, 1954. On the policy of al-Nasir: A. Hartmann, *An-Nasir li-Din Allah*, Berlin, 1975.

Chapter 6 Centres of civilisation

On architectural forms see *EI*[1], article: Masdjid (J. Pedersen) to be supplemented by more recent studies, especially: J. Sauvaget, *La Mosquée omeyyade de Médine*, Paris, 1947; J. Sourdel-Thomine, 'La Mosquée et la madrasa', *Cahiers de civilisation médiévale*, 13 (1970), 97–115; K. A. C. Creswell, *Muslim Architecture of Egypt*, Oxford, 1952–9; L. Hautecoeur, *Les Mosquées du Caire*, Paris, 1932; J. Sourdel-Thomine, 'Deux minarets d'époque seldjoukide en Afghanistan', *Syria*, 30 (1953), 108–36; *EI*[2], articles: Bimaristan, Hammam; K. A. C. Creswell, *Early Muslim Architecture*, 2nd edn, Oxford, 1969 (on palaces and mosques); D. Schlumberger and J. Sourdel-Thomine, *Lashkari Bazar*, I, Paris, 1978; J. Sauvaget, 'La citadelle de Damas', *Syria*, II (1930), 59–90, 216–41, and 'Caravansérails syriens du Moyen Age', *Ars Islamica*, 6 (1939), 48–55 and 7 (1940), 1–19; K. Erdmann, *Das anatolische Karavansaray des 13. Jahrhunderts*, Berlin, 1961.

On palace ceremonial: M. Canard, 'Le cérémonial fatimide et le cérémonial byzantin; essai de comparaison', *Byzantion*, 21 (1951), 356–420; D. Sourdel, 'Questions de cérémonial 'abbaside', *REI*, 28 (1960), 121–48; on entertainments: M. Canard, 'Quelques aspects de la vie sociale en Syrie et Jazira au Xe siècle', in *Arabic and Islamic Studies*, Leiden, 1965, 168–90.

On art: B. Spuler and J. Sourdel-Thomine, *Die Kunst des Islam*, Berlin, 1973, and J. Sourdel-Thomine, 'Introduction à l'art de l'islam', *REI*, 43 (1975), 3–44, 195–225 (French version of the text of the above work); J. Sourdel-Thomine, 'Arts et société dans le monde de l'islam', *REI*, 36 (1968), 93–114; D. Talbot Rice, *Islamic Art*, London, 1965; O. Grabar, *The Formation of Islamic Art*, New Haven, 1976.

On relations between Islam and the West: W. Montgomery Watt, *The Influence of Islam on Medieval Europe*, Edinburgh, 1972; G. Makdisi, *The Rise of Colleges* (above), and 'Interaction between Islam and the West', *REI*, 44 (1976), 287–309.

Index

Note Names prefixed by 'al-' appear in strict alphabetical order under 'al-'.

Index

Index